Trigger High Performance

Upgrade Your Mind, Learn Effectively to Become an Expert, Activate Flow State to Take Relentless Action, and Perform At Your Best

SOM BATHLA

www.sombathla.com

Your Free Gift

As a token of my thanks for taking out time to read my book, I would like to offer you a free gift:

Click Below and Download your **Free Report**

Learn 5 Mental Shifts To Turbo-Charge Your Performance In Every Area Of Your Life - in Next 30 Days!

You can also grab your FREE GIFT Report through this below URL:

http://sombathla.com/mentalshifts

Table of Contents

Introduction 4

Chapter 1: Why High Performance is Accessible to Anyone 10

Chapter 2: Recreate Your Self-Image to Activate High Performance 23

Chapter 3: Activate These Mental Shifts to Upgrade Your Thinking 36

Chapter 4: How to Acquire and Upgrade Skills Effectively 60

Chapter 5: Build Expertise and Attain Mastery in Anything You Do 80

Chapter 6: Science-Backed Ways to Boost Willpower for Focused Performance 92

Chapter 7: How to Activate High Performance in Everyday Life 113

Chapter 8: The Neuroscience of the "Flow" State and How to Experience it More Often 127

Closing Thoughts 143

May I ask you for a small favor? 145

Full Book Summary 146

Preview of the book "Intelligent Thinking" 163

My Books in Personal Mastery Series 173

Introduction

****

"Peak performance begins with your taking complete responsibility for your life and everything that happens to you."

~ *Brian Tracy*

For Jenny, it was not just a regular day at the office.

Along with her other colleagues, she would receive her long-awaited performance appraisal results. Jenny was a bit nervous, frequently glancing at her watch and then towards the cabin of her marketing head. The marketing department she worked in was buzzing more than usual. Jenny observed her colleagues as they entered and left her boss's office — they spent *fifteen to twenty* minutes in there. Some co-workers looked elated (as if they had been promoted), while others seemed only content (as if they had been awarded normal salary hikes). A few of her co-workers appeared frustrated or upset (as if they had experienced something serious, such as reprimands).

Suddenly, her heart started beating faster than usual, as it was her turn. Jenny would enter that corner room in only a few minutes; she was anxious, and her palms were drenched in sweat.

Eventually, she was called in. Her reporting manager, a tall, handsome man in his early forties, and an HR representative from her organization were sitting on the opposite side of a big table. Jenny took her seat, and after exchanging brief greetings, they began to discuss her appraisal and feedback with her.

She began to realize that her anxiety and fears were not entirely unfounded; Jenny received feedback that her performance was not up to the mark, and the organization wanted her to gear up faster and strengthen her competencies and skill set to better address her job requirements. At length, she received a letter that offered an average three-star performance rating (five stars were given only to top performers) with only a marginal salary hike. Deeply sad and frustrated, Jenny left the room and somehow managed to reach her cubicle.

Sitting dejectedly at her desk, she began to reflect on what had just occurred. She thought of all her colleagues who had cheerfully and excitedly exited her boss's office — and, more particularly, about Zara. Zara, who was one of the smartest young women in Jenny's marketing team, had left the boss's office beaming victoriously. In the next few minutes, Jenny was at Zara's workstation, inquiring about her performance appraisal. Jenny had guessed correctly: Zara was promoted to the next level and got a decent salary hike.

After congratulating Zara and managing, with some difficulty, to finish her urgent work, Jenny called it a day and left the office early. At home, she recollected and reflected upon past instances of Zara's outstanding performance; Jenny realized that in the few short years she had worked with her, Zara had always enjoyed more freedom at work because she delivered exceptional results, regardless of the tasks assigned to her. She was given much more independence while dealing with the organizations' clients and a great deal of flexibility to schedule meetings with clients at her convenience. Also, although Zara seemed to be consistently given more work responsibilities, she never appeared to be stressed or anxious about the work — she remained calm and continued to deliver stellar results to the organization. Zara's promotion was well-deserved.

Then Jenny began to reflect on her own working life. She realized that she felt anxious, mostly about work and about what her superiors thought of her. Jenny always felt swamped with work, despite having much less work than Zara and although she was almost always the last one to leave office regularly.

Obviously, she was overwhelmed and frustrated about what had happened that day, but she was also curious. Her head was reeling with questions, such as:

- What made Zara deliver such amazing results despite having more work under her belt than herself?
- How come Zara could work tirelessly and seemingly without any stress, despite being loaded with highly demanding clients?
- Did Zara acquire those high-performance traits by birth, or did she up her game by learning and practicing the tricks of the trade?
- Was there some secret recipe for her exceptional performance — one that allowed Zara to lead a successful and happy life?

In this modern, highly competitive, and demanding world, almost everyone — not only Jenny — is curious to know how high performers do what they do while the rest of the world struggles.

Like Jenny, most people in business, sports, or other fields would love to have the secret recipes that high achievers use in every part of their lives to succeed consistently and wonder:

- What makes some people crush it in every field, while most individuals just struggle hard to escape their mediocre lives?

- What makes such people master their body and mind and always seem beaming with grace despite handling high-stake responsibilities?

And the most important of all the questions that any high-performance enthusiast (yours truly included) should look for answer is:

- ***How can an individual attain that physical and mental state where he or she can consistently, and over a long period of time, perform at higher levels and deliver extraordinary results?***

As someone who is always researching and implementing ways to improve my mindset, behavior, and performance, I assure that you are in the right place to find the answer to this question.

This book's objective is to address the above question — and to do so, we will delve deeper into neuroscience, human psychology, and behavioral studies/researches to isolate the principles of high performance followed by ultra-achievers in different fields of their lives.

The real-life examples in the book will inspire and offer you explicit evidence of how these principles have been implemented by successful people in all fields of life, be it sports, arts, or business, to deliver the highest level of performance for a longer sustainable period.

This book is about the long-term strategies that talk about your inner mindset, the science of how your body and mind works, and how you can start applying the principles as you read them. This book is not about some quick hacks or tactics with short-lived performance boosters; rather, it focuses on a long-term sustainable approach to change your mindset and presents a different way of performing your tasks and achieving your wildly important goals.

Throughout this book, I will share simple, but highly effective, principles, along with some real-life examples of high achievers. I assure you that by the time you put the book down, your mind will have already digested many mental principles that will help trigger your next actions. Once you implement these principles in your life, you will undoubtedly enhance your performance muscles and progress faster towards your highest goals.

With that assurance, I ask you to join this short journey of learning the tools of high performance to significantly improve the quality of your life.

Let's get started!

Chapter 1: Why High Performance is Accessible to Anyone

****

"I have always believed that everyone has the potential to do something extraordinary if they're guided and helped along the way."

~ Bob Mathias

What is High Performance?

Before we dig deeper into how to achieve a state of high performance, let's first understand what the term high performance means. As per the Cambridge dictionary, high performance is **the ability to operate to a high standard and at a high speed.**

Another definition, from the Collins Dictionary[1], explains high performance by referring to a

---

[1] https://www.collinsdictionary.com/dictionary/english/high-performance

high-performance car or another product that goes very fast or does a lot. Then it finally defines high performance as **very efficient and powerful.**

I resonate with the definition of high performance by Brendon Burchard, which states: **"high performance is consistently performing and delivering results above and beyond standard norms over the long-term."**

Three pre-requisites of high performance that emerge from all the above definitions are:

- One must **deliver beyond the normal standards**, i.e. a standard much higher than the normal.
- The results should be **delivered in a faster way**.
- One should be able to deliver such results **consistently over the long term.**

How High Performance is Accessible to Everyone

You might have heard people raving about someone who they felt was gifted with some talent. A vast majority of people still think that all high achievers have genetically acquired their abilities.

But unfortunately, due to this reasoning, they rule out the possibility that they could perform at those levels and achieve that kind of success.

And what happens next?

Yes, you guessed correctly: with such a false belief system, most individuals don't even try something new or different. And the reason they give for not trying is that a few selected people are gifted, but they are not — so why even attempt new things and waste their time?

But if you explore the lives of such high achievers further — those who you think have succeeded because they have natural abilities or gifts — you will be surprised to learn that most of them have spent significant parts of their lives developing their competencies and skills to perform at much higher levels and generate massive results.

As T. Harv Eker said, *"Every master was once a disaster."* Barring a few child prodigies, most high achievers have paid the price of success by putting in their blood, sweat and tears to earn glorious success. These go-getters have dedicated themselves to intensive training that drives changes in the brain and body, making it possible for them to achieve things that they couldn't have done otherwise.

Of course, it is not possible to change everything; genetic constraints exist. You cannot expect a five-foot person to master the game of basketball, as they would be at a disadvantage when compared to taller players. Similarly, you cannot expect a statuesque woman to comfortably master gymnastics.

But here is the good news for most people: barring a few genetic constraints, for the most part, the human body and mind can be stated **as a normalizing machine**. If you expose humans to a different set of environments or circumstances, they will face some initial internal resistance, but over time, the new environment starts appearing normal. **Our mind tends to become normalized to a new environment through consistent exposure**.

Let's look at an example. Assume you are an overweight person. If you start going to the gym for an hour a day each morning or evening, you will see and meet people who are physically fit and have optimal weight. Initially, you may be reluctant to run on the treadmill or lift weights, but over time, you will become acclimatized to the new environment. Now, if you continue in that environment for some time, you will start getting inspired by the healthy and fit people around you. Suddenly, losing weight — which seemed a difficult task earlier — now seems to be within reach, thanks to your exposure to a new environment.

This concept of the normalization of human beings is one of the most important features of human ability. Once you are convinced of this concept, you would not limit yourself by simply ruling out possibilities by dismissing them as the result of luck or inborn talent.

Two Scientific Principles That Make Humans Highly Adaptable

The principles of homeostasis and neuroplasticity are responsible for human adaptability. Let's review them one by one.

Homeostasis: Our bodies can adapt to anything.

Homeostasis is a key concept that explains how our body functions. The word homeostasis is formed with two Greek words: '**homeo**', meaning 'similar', and '**stasis**', meaning 'stable'.

A more formal definition of homeostasis is **a characteristic of a system that regulates its internal environment and tends to maintain a stable, relatively constant condition of properties.**

To put it more simply, homeostasis means a system's tendency to do what it needs to do to maintain stability. Let's look at how it applies to the system of our body and mind.

Every cell in our body and brain is *constantly* working to maintain a sense of stability — adjusting everything from our blood pressure and heart rate to our pH balance and blood sugar levels. Our body wants to keep things stable and normal at a particular level all the time.

Therefore, whenever we push ourselves beyond what is comfortable for our bodies, our bodies respond by overcompensating in the pursuit of creating a new higher level of homeostasis.

That's the reason that any kind of physical activity creates changes in the body: when a body system — certain muscles, the cardiovascular system, or any other muscle — are stressed to the point that homeostasis can no longer be maintained, the body responds with changes that are intended to re-establish homeostasis.

For example, if you start lifting weights at the gym more often than usual, your body will ask you, *"What are you doing? You're pushing me out of homeostasis. Let me see what I can do to handle this new load and calibrate a new level of homeostasis."*

The law of homeostasis applies everywhere; it applies to running more miles today than you did yesterday, learning a new language, playing guitar, or anything else that you desire. You have an existing level of comfort or skill or stability in what you do. **Whenever you expose yourself to new environments and stretch yourself beyond your routine, your body and mind improve their homeostasis and establish a new standard.**

This amazing story of Swedish adventurer Göran Kropp is an excellent example of how human bodies can adapt to any situation through this normalizing capacity governed by the principle of homeostasis. In October 1995, Kropp started his journey from Stockholm, Sweden, on his bicycle; he rode all the way and reached the base of the Himalayas in April 1996. Surprisingly, Kropp didn't take any oxygen mask with him; nor did he seek the help of any Sherpa (local people who know the mountain routes and accompany the mountaineers). Without an oxygen mask or any other person's help, this brave man reached the summit of Mount Everest on his own. After touching the apex of the mountain, Kropp then descended normally, picked up his bike, and peddled back to Sweden — making it look easy.

Although this would surely seem a life-threatening adventure for anyone, Kropp did this. That's the power of the adaptability of our bodies.

Let's examine another example of the adaptability and limitlessness of human potential. If anyone asks you how many miles someone can run in one stretch, some of you may guess about a marathon's length — or maybe a little longer. Remember, I am talking about running in one single stretch without taking any breaks.

You would be amazed to learn that a tribe called T*arahumara*, the Native American people of north-western Mexico, can run up to an astonishing two hundred miles in one spurt. Isn't it amazing to witness what the human body is capable of when we push ourselves to the limit?

Now let's talk about another concept that is related more specifically to the human mind's capacity to adapt and change as per the environment and circumstances it gets exposed to frequently.

Neuroplasticity: How Human Minds are Malleable

The concept of neuroplasticity is all about the plasticity of our minds. Neuroscience has proven that our brains are malleable and can be molded into entirely something different.

Neuroplasticity is an umbrella term referring to the ability of your brain to reorganize itself, both physically and functionally, throughout your life due to your environment, behavior, thoughts, and emotions. Science has proven that radical improvements in cognitive function — how we learn, think, perceive, and remember — are possible even in the elderly; these changes can happen regardless of age.

Therefore, **the good news is that your brain makes physical changes based on the repetitive things you do and the experiences you have**. The bad news is that your brain makes physical changes based on the repetitive things you do and the experiences you have. Therefore, this morphing capability of your brain, known as neuroplasticity, works both for you and against you. Therefore, if you choose to expose your mind to positive people and positive environments, take growth-oriented actions, and avoid indulgences and instant gratification, you can use the power of neuroplasticity to your advantage.

This is a really exciting feature of the human brain; in fact, it's our greatest gift. We need to use it wisely, as we can stretch ourselves beyond our falsely set up mental thresholds, which have kept us from performing exceptionally well and reaching our true potential.

A Real-Life Example of How Neuroplasticity Can Grow Your Brain

The miraculous life story of a little girl named Cameron Mott[2], from North Carolina, proves

---
[2] https://www.theconfidentteacher.com/2017/09/a-new-school-year-and-a-new-start/

the enormous impact of neuroplasticity on our brain's abilities. Just after her third birthday, Cameron started having violent seizures; they became worse, and eventually, she lost her ability to speak. Doctors diagnosed her with Rasmussen's encephalitis, a rare inflammatory neurological disease, and the only treatment was hemispherectomy — removing half of her brain.

The impact of this surgery would be very catastrophic for this girl because one half of your brain is responsible for and controls movement and sensation in the other half of your body, i.e. the left hemisphere controls the right side of your entire body's function and vice versa. This surgery would immediately leave Cameron hemiplegic, meaning that she would suffer from paralysis on one side of the body.

But to everyone's utmost surprise, just four weeks post-operation, she walked out of the hospital. And after a few months of difficult rehabilitation, she returned to good health and was again going to school, participating in school activities, and living a life of miraculous normality. She was free from seizures after the surgery, and despite having half of her brain removed, she was able to live a normal life.

How could 50% of the brain work almost like 100% for Cameron?

It happened because the remaining part of Cameron's brain sensed the massive loss of neural tissue, and it physically rewired and reorganized itself to take over everything that the other half had previously handled. This proves the vast ability of the brain to change itself — to rewire.

The above stories prove that human bodies and minds are highly adaptable. Therefore, you must realize that we have no shortage of capabilities. We excessively doubt ourselves, and acquired patterns of negative thinking amassed from our surroundings. One must take an entirely different approach to seek the benefits of the concept of homeostasis and neuroplasticity. The above examples are extreme ones, but convey a strong message about the limitlessness of human potential. So, we need to overcome our limiting beliefs, rise above our fears, and get ready to perform to the best of our abilities.

Your upper limits are unknown and unknowable. Only you can go further and test out your limits; no one else can do it for you.

With deliberate practice, the objective is not merely to reach your potential but to build it, to make things possible that were not possible before. This requires challenging homeostasis — frequently coming out of your comfort zone — and forcing your brain or your body to adapt. But once you do this, learning becomes a way of taking control of your life and shaping your potential in the ways you want to do so.

The principles of homeostasis and neuroplasticity give us the irrefutable proof that human capabilities are not fixed or established by the time of our birth; they prove that regardless of whatever environment we are raised in, irrespective of our parents, teachers, and friends, we can always stretch and move beyond what we are.

Chapter 1: Key Takeaways

High performance, as astutely defined by Brendon Burchard, is consistently performing and delivering results above and beyond standard norms over the long-term.

High performers are not necessarily the ones who become so because of genetics or their natural talent. Human biology is governed by certain principles that enable anyone to excel in their performance.

Barring a few genetic constraints, for the most part, the human body and mind can be very well stated **as a normalizing machine**. If, over time, you expose humans to a different set of environments or circumstances, they can adapt and perform in any circumstances. Two principles that govern this human adaptability are:

- **Homeostasis:**

Homeostasis is a characteristic of a system that regulates its internal environment and tends to maintain a stable, relatively constant condition of properties.

When we push ourselves beyond what is comfortable for our bodies, our bodies respond by overcompensating in the pursuit of creating a new higher level of homeostasis.

- **Neuroplasticity**

Neuroplasticity refers to the **ability of the human brain to reorganize itself, both physically and functionally, due to your environment, behavior, thinking, and emotions** — irrespective of age, gender, demography, location, etc.

The principles of homeostasis and neuroplasticity give enough confidence that our bodies and brains are capable of performing well beyond our self-created false limits. By merely becoming aware of these principles, helps anyone to start thinking differently about themselves and their capacities.

Chapter 2: Recreate Your Self-Image to Activate High Performance

****

"A strong, positive self-image is the best possible preparation for success in life."

– Dr. Joyce Brothers

In the previous section, you learned about the adaptability of the human body and brain by the principles of homeostasis and neuroplasticity. Once you understand that you don't have any limits, rather that you limit yourself by the false limits created by you and only you, it gives you a sense of liberation.

But here, it is pertinent to mention that despite being aware of many wonderful principles, we humans don't necessarily benefit from them. For example, everyone knows that exercise is good for physical and mental health, but most people don't get out of their comfy beds in the morning or leave their cushy couches to hit the gym.

Why is it so?

This is because people form their self-images based on their upbringing, environment, or frequent past behaviors. Once they form self-images, it becomes difficult for them to take any action that doesn't fit into their self-defined persona. For example, if you have formed a self-image as a shy person who avoids talking to strangers or as a lazy person who has always come up with excuses to avoid working out, this self-image will outrightly reject those activities that don't fit with this falsely created self-image.

Your self-image plays a vital role in how you approach any activity and thus affects your performance. Your level of performance will be limited to the level that you see yourself as capable of. You would never perform beyond what you see yourself capable of achieving.

Therefore, in this chapter, let's learn about the concept of self-image and how we can change our self-image to improve our performance.

There is a broader term known as **self-concept,** and one of the subsets of that is self-image. Carl Rogers, an American psychologist, believes that the **self-concept has three different components**:

- The view you have of yourself **(self-image)**

- How much value you place on yourself **(self-esteem or self-worth)**
- What you wish you were like **(ideal self)**

Here, we will talk only about the first component, i.e. self-image. Jason Selk, one of the premier performance coaches in the United States, defines self-image as below:

"Self-image is essentially how you view yourself — what strengths and weaknesses you believe you possess and what you believe you are capable of achieving."

Jason compares your self-image to a thermostat and explains how your performance can never exceed the self-image you have established for yourself. He states:

Essentially, the self-image governs how successful any individual becomes because it motivates and shapes an individual's work ethic and effort. In this way, self-image is like a thermostat; if you set the thermostat at 72 degrees Fahrenheit, and the room drops to 71 degrees, the thermostat then sends a message to the heater to get to work. Warm air rushes into the room, and the room warms up to 72 degrees. When the room reaches 73 degrees, the thermostat tells the heater to stop working. All day long, the thermostat governs the temperature in the room and won't allow the room temperature to rise or drop from the desired temperature for long.

Human beings are the same way: we neither outperform nor underperform our self-image for long. That's why it is so important to set your self-image gauge high enough to achieve your life goals. Set your self-image gauge too low, and you'll underachieve because your mind won't call for the motivation to achieve more.

Therefore, it becomes even more important to first take a close look at how we see ourselves. Once we can see ourselves as capable of completing a particular task, then our action will be aligned with our identity. As someone once stated: ***"Your Identity precedes Activity".***

How to Ascertain Your Self-Image?

If you have some difficulty identifying your true self-image, there are some tools that can hold your hand and lead you to the relevant questions that will help you to determine your self-image.

In 1954, Manfred Kuhn, a social psychologist, developed a tool known as **The Twenty Statements Test (TST)**[3], which he used to

---

[3] http://psychology.wikia.com/wiki/Twenty_Statements_Test

delve deeper into the self-image. He would ask people to answer the question "Who am I?" in 20 different ways, and in the process, he realized that the responses could be divided into two major groups: (1) ***social roles*** (external or objective aspects of oneself such as son, teacher, or friend) and (2) ***personality traits*** (internal or affective aspects of oneself such as sympathetic, impatient, or humorous).

The list of answers to the question "Who Am I?" includes examples of each of the following four types of responses:

1. **Physical Description**: I'm tall, I have blue eyes, etc.

2. **Social Roles:** We are all social beings, and our behavior is shaped, to some extent, by the roles we play. Roles such as student, housewife, or sports team member help others to recognize us. At the same time, these roles help us to know what is expected of us in various situations.

3. **Personal Traits:** This is another dimension of our self-description. You might describe your personal traits in the following way: "I'm impulsive, I'm generous, and I tend to worry a lot".

4. **Existential Statements** (abstract ones): These can range from: "I'm a child of the universe" to "I'm a human being" to "I'm a spiritual being", etc.

Depending upon your age, social connections, relationships, and your behaviors, your answers to these questions will vary. You will realize that answering these questions will help you to see your self-image in a broader sense — and that realization itself will provide you with valuable insight into why you perform a particular task in your own particular way or avoid taking some action.

For example, if your self-image whispers in your head, "I am a shy guy". Now, you can easily imagine how your behavior would be if you had to attend a party. Your first thought would be to find an excuse not to go. And even if you go to the party, you will stand in a corner and do your best to find a way to get out of the place as soon as you can. That's the power of self-image, which governs all your behaviors and actions in any situation.

Okay, what should we do next?

I suggest spending some time in quiet reflection to assess how you perceive your self-image. Also, don't assume that your self-image is the same throughout your entire life. It is rather fluid and keeps on changing subtly and gradually as you grow up and get exposed to different types of environments. If you think that it is your self-image that is not supporting you to deliver high-performance in your pursuits, then it is time to change your self-image.

How to Change Your Self-Image to Boost Your Performance

If you realize that you are not able to perform or take charge of your life, it's time to change your self-image, which is quite possible to do. It can be stated with certainty that everything changes. You have learned already the concepts of homeostasis and neuroplasticity that support the idea that your body and brain change.

Therefore, the good part about modifying your self-image is that it is not that hard to do. The principles through which your current self-image is formed in a restricted manner can be applied intentionally when you want to build a much-liberated self-image.

The only difference is that earlier you allowed your self-image to form naturally (thanks to outside exposures) — and now you must control the process of remodeling your self-image.

Lanny Bassham, an American sports shooter and an Olympic gold medalist, gives his personal example in his book and suggests the ways through which anyone can change their self-image. Bassham claims to have spoken to hundreds of Olympic athletes and PGA tour pros about their secrets of high performance. And every one of them had answered unequivocally that **at least 90% of their game was mental**.

Therefore, his formula for changing your self-image is through mental training, and this mental training serves dual purposes: first, the practice involves personal statements designed to get you to see yourself as an achiever, and second, it includes mentally practicing the performance at the highest level. His mental training formula, which serves these dual objectives, has two components:

1. **Mental Rehearsal**

This mental rehearsal is not like your vision boards showing the marvelous outcomes like plush dream homes, fancy cars, or foreign travels, etc. It is not about the visualization of you already having achieved the results. **It is all about the process of taking action towards getting the results**. In this approach, you mentally rehearse performing that task in the most effective way, see yourself making the perfect move, and see yourself succeeding always.

Combine the personal statement below with this element of mental rehearsal.

2. **A personal statement:** *"I do it all the time." + "That's like me."*

Now this personal statement is a game-changer; it imprints your new identity of high performance in your brain. This is not some mystical statement; it is based on neuroscience and, more specifically, the concept of neuroplasticity is based on this principle that our minds are molded by our environment, behavior, thinking, and emotions.

In his book, *With Winning in Mind: The Mental Management System,* Lanny shares his personal example of how only with the help of the mental training as explained above — and without much physical training — he was able to win athletic competitions. He states that before he won the Olympic gold, he was in the Army. He was stationed somewhere that was two hundred and fifty miles away from a shooting range. So, in those two years, he was only able to shoot for six days, and those were during competitions—three days for one national competition and three days for another.

He explains that after his family went to bed, he'd spend two to four hours a night, five nights a week, imagining he was shooting. In this mental rehearsal, he practiced in his mind precisely that he was standing in the correct posture, aiming the point, and then finally shooting precisely at the destination. And surprisingly, he won both of those national competitions with the help of these mental rehearsals.

That's the power of building a high performer's self-image and combining it with a mental rehearsal of your best performance.

Psychologist and researcher Heidi Grant-Halvorson, in her book Succeed: How We Can Reach Our Goals, shares the view that instead of solely visualizing a successful outcome (which she bluntly rejects), one should visualize the process of achieving success. Here is what she said:

"What about "visualizing success"? I won't name names, but it seems like there are an awful lot of self-help books out there telling people that if they just picture what they want in their minds, it will somehow happen. That would be great if it were true, but scientifically speaking, there isn't much evidence for it. On the other hand, **visualization can be very helpful if you imagine the steps you will take in order to succeed, rather than the success itself.** *Mentally simulating the process of achieving the goal, rather than the hoped-for outcome, not only results in a more optimistic outlook but greater planning and*

preparation. **Picture yourself doing what it takes to succeed, and you will soon find yourself believing that you can.*"*

Surround Yourself with People Who Believe in You.

If you have watched *The Matrix,* you can relate to this example: how Morpheus (played by Laurence Fishburne) kept telling Neo (played by Keanu Reeves) that he was "the one" despite Neo doubting his ability to crack the Matrix code. But Morpheus placed so much trust in Neo that, ultimately, Neo started to believe that he was "the one", and he gained full access to his potential.

That's the magic of someone believing in you — it gives you the consistent reinforcement of your abilities.

There is no dearth of potential in any human being; rather, our fears and doubts cripple us. Therefore, you should become friends with folks who believe in creating and designing their life because their company will elevate you. You'll get the shoulder-rubbing effect by spending some time with them. These individuals can be friends, mentors, or coaches — people who believe in you and your ability to achieve things in life. If they are coaches, they are invested in your success because it's only your results that will prove their mettle.

Don't spend time with people who don't trust you; they create an environment of fear and negativity around you. If that person happens to be your spouse or close relative, then don't try to prove your beliefs to them; rather, avoid arguing with them.

You must be careful enough in trying to inspire other people only to the extent that it doesn't start negatively influencing you.

Now, in the next chapter, let's delve into the tools and strategies that will pave the way to your best performance.

Chapter 2: Key Takeaways

Despite being aware of the principle of the malleability of our human bodies and brains, most people fail to make the changes necessary to lead a better life.

The key reason why people fail to transform is their self-image. They can't act beyond what they perceive as their own self-image, and they run their lives based on the identities they have created for themselves.

Your identity precedes your activity.

Your self-image can be divided into two parts (1) Social roles; and (2) Personality Traits, as identified by social psychologist, Manfred Kuhn.

If your self-image is not serving, and you fail to take charge of your life, it's time to change your life.

Lanny Bassham, Olympic Gold Medalist in shooting and a high-performance enthusiast based on his talks with hundreds of sports personalities, concluded that **all the high performers attribute 90% of their success to the mental game**. He proposes a two-part formula to change your self-image, as per below:

- **Mental Rehearsal**

In this approach, you mentally rehearse performing that task in the most effective way, see yourself making the perfect move, and see yourself succeeding always.

- **A personal statement:** *"I do it all the time."* + *"That's like me."*

These affirmation statements imprint your new identity of high performance in your brain.

Surround yourself with people who evoke a sense of faith in you, and minimize the time you spend with negative people.

Chapter 3: Activate These Mental Shifts to Upgrade Your Thinking

****

"Progress is impossible without change, and those who cannot change their minds cannot change anything."

~ George Bernard Shaw

Our brains are psychologically wired to be biased towards negativity. Negativity bias[4] implies behavior that despite carrying equal intensity, things of a more negative nature (e.g. unpleasant thoughts, emotions, social interaction, or harmful/traumatic events) have a greater effect on one's psychological state and processes than neutral or positive things.

In other words, something positive will generally have less of an impact on a person's behavior and cognition than something equally emotional but negative.

If we don't voluntarily control our thoughts and emotions, these tiny invisible creatures carry a

---

[4] https://en.wikipedia.org/wiki/Negativity_bias

huge power to ruin our mental state, thus generating a negative behavior leading to non-performance or performance at a low or below-average level.

But hang on! Don't jump to conclusions so quickly because the best part is that humans are gifted with consciousness (unlike other animals), which means that we do have the power to exercise control on our thoughts. Unfortunately, most people rarely do anything to change the direction of their thoughts — they think and believe that they don't have any choice but to get swayed by any random thoughts popping up in their heads.

However, a very small percentage of people, who are growth-mindset oriented and sincerely care about unleashing their full potential and performing at their best, choose to control their thoughts. Since I'm creating this book and you are reading it, both of us fall into this small percentage of people, so let's give ourselves a pat on our back (I just did; do it, too, and then continue reading).

Okay, now let's talk about what we are going to cover next. In this section, you will learn about a few mental shifts — ways to transform your thinking patterns — that will help you to overcome your negativity bias and empower you to transform yourself into a driven action-taker.

I call them mental shifts and not merely changes because a shift means a major transformation and not some minor tweak or modification. These mental shifts, backed by studies and experiments by psychology researchers, have the potential to rewire your thinking patterns, leading to energized emotion and behavior followed by massive actions. And guess what happens? You will start getting amazing results sooner.

So, let's get straight into these mental shifts.

Take Stress as a Challenge, Not a Threat

Unfortunately, most people view stress as a threat — something they should avoid. But that's not the way high performers view stress. All successful people who perform at a high level consider stress as a challenge; they don't get threatened — rather, they feel challenged.

Hans Selye, an Austrian endocrinologist who is known for critical scientific work on an organism's response to stressors and the effects of stress on the human body, coined the term "**Eustress**". You can see here that the term stress is prefixed by 'Eu', which is a Greek word that means 'good'. Therefore, Eustress means good or beneficial stress.

If you consider any kind of stress to be a challenge, then you expose your mind to a beneficial emotion called Eustress. Researchers call this response a *challenge response*, which is characterized by viewing stress as something positive — and merely by considering it positively, it becomes a growth stimulus.

Amid stress, people who demonstrate the challenge response focus proactively on the things they can control. With that shift in focus to what you can control, your mind releases a different set of chemicals, generating positive emotions that trigger appropriate behavior and action enabling you to take charge of any situation, rather than making you feel anxious or worried about that situation. If you take any situation as a challenge, then you'll be focused on dissecting the problem into controllable and uncontrollable aspects. This mental shift means demonstrating the challenge response, which means taking appropriate actions during controllable situations (like working extra hours to finish a project), but at the same time, this brings you at peace with the uncontrollable things (e.g. any natural calamity, major policy changes etc.) and reduces unnecessary worry and anxiety.

Eustress, or the challenge response, is not only motivational or inspirational advice; rather, it is properly backed by neuroscience about the release of supportive brain chemicals to encourage your positive actions.

As per neuroscience, when someone shifts their beliefs and considers stress as a challenge to conquer, their mind releases more of DHEA (Dehydroepiandrosterone), a hormone also classified as a neurosteroid. DHEA strengthens your brain when you face psychological challenges.

Now the key point here is that if you view stress as a challenge and want to face it, only then will you get a supply of DHEA. For example, if you are participating in any adventurous sport, you are taking it as a challenge, and, therefore, it will trigger the release of DHEA from your brain. But if you think of stress as a threat, your mind will release another chemical called cortisol, a stress hormone that is responsible to handle any threat. You'll experience an increase in heart rate and blood pressure upon perceiving a threat. You might experience this when you suddenly get exposed to some dangerous situations.

The ratio of DHEA to cortisol that you release during stress is sometimes referred to as the *growth index*[5] of your stress response. A higher growth index — meaning more DHEA relative to cortisol — is associated with thriving

---

[5] http://onlinelibrary.wiley.com/doi/10.1111/j.1540-4560.1998.tb01220.x/abstract

during and after stressful experiences. Those who view stress as a challenge — and not as a threat — have this optimal ratio.

There was a study conducted on swimmers by dividing them into two different groups and seeing how these two groups considered stress, i.e. as a challenge or a threat. The results of the study showed that the non-elites viewed stress as something to avoid, ignore, and try to eliminate; they felt that stress would hurt their performance. The elites, on the other hand, interpreted the stress and the sensations that came with it as an aid to their performance; it prepared them to get the most out of their bodies.

Studies[6] confirm that viewing a stressful situation as an opportunity to improve your skills, knowledge, or strengths makes it more likely that you will experience stress inoculation or stress-related growth.

Stress-relieving expert Dr. Robert Eliot, in his book, *Dare to Be 100*, suggests that one should work with stress instead of running away from it. He suggests that the central ingredient in building familiarity with stress is your perspective on it. If you view every miniature departure from your routine environment as a threat leading to major adverse consequences, then life is going to be arduous for you.

---

[6] https://www.ncbi.nlm.nih.gov/pubmed/23478676

I loved his simple formula to beat stress, and it's worth remembering as a brain tattoo. He says:

"First, don't sweat the little things, and second, everything is a little thing."

Once you appreciate that going through stress makes you better at it, it gets easier to face each new challenge. And the expectation of growth sends a signal to your brain and body: get ready to learn something because you can handle this.

Carnegie's Four-Step Formula to Beat 90% of Stress

This is the age of getting results at lightning speed. We want quick solutions. Thankfully, there is a formula for dealing with stress as well. Dale Carnegie gave a straightforward piece of advice on how to deal with stress through a four-step formula. In his own words:

*"Experience has proved to me, time after time, the enormous value of arriving at a decision. It is the failure to arrive at a fixed purpose, the inability to stop going round and round in maddening circles... I find that **fifty percent of my worries vanish once I arrive at a clear decision, and another forty percent usually vanish once I start to carry out that decision**.*

> *So, I banish about **ninety percent of my worries by taking these four steps**:*

1. *Writing down precisely what I am worried about.*
2. *Writing down what I can do about it.*
3. *Deciding what to do.*
4. *Starting immediately to carry out that decision.*

Therefore, don't get stressed; rather, work with stress. Take stress as a challenge to steal the benefits of neurochemistry with the help of the right hormones. Carnegie's formula puts it in more simple terms to help you make this mental shift.

So let's move to the next mental shift.

Consistent Thought Replacement

Take any area of your life where you want to excel, and you will realize that the people you are competing with are equally qualified and have the required skill set and experience to deliver elite performances.

Take the corporate world — you will find that most people possess the requisite qualifications, experience, and necessary skill sets to deliver the job. In fact, they form the key criteria that HR representatives establish before recruiting any person for a particular position. In the world of sports, most athletes go through a similar set of physical training, diets, or exercising schedule.

You can take any other area of life, but the common theme that you'd observe is that the threshold qualifications, skill sets, and experience fall into a similar range when we compare different people. Still, you see only a handful of those people demonstrate excellence in their performance.

Have you ever wondered why that is so? **Why do only a few individuals outshine others, when most are qualified and have developed skill sets by spending years gaining experiences?** What is so special about elite performers?

Here is their secret: they consistently follow thought replacement, replacing any negative thoughts with positive and helpful ones.

High performers train their minds to choose the most resourceful thought at any particular moment. Jason Selk, a performance coach in the US, in his book *10-Minute Toughness,* talks about the **level of efficiency at which high performers observe and choose their thoughts.** He goes on to explain that any given point of time, you must consistently keep weighing whether the thoughts going on in your mind are supporting your performance or hurting it. He stated:

"If you determine what you want to accomplish in any given situation, <u>then lock your mind on</u>

what it takes to achieve that goal, you will have a much better chance of reaping the rewards.

This is true in any setting—business, sport, or even social. As often as possible, choose to think about the path to success rather than the obstacles in your way. You have to decide what you want and then put your energy into acquiring it. Don't wait for good luck to find you. Go out and create your luck. **The only reliable method for overcoming self-doubt and negative thinking is to supply something else for your mind to process.** *In my opinion, the essence of mental toughness is the ability to replace negative thinking with thoughts that are centered on performance cues or that contribute to improved self-confidence."*

Therefore, the key tenet of thought replacement is **to consistently observe your thoughts and always direct them towards your desired goal**; don't let your mind wander by indulging in negative thoughts, reflecting on criticism, or getting swept up by mere distractions.

You already know that, in any sport, the difference between a winner and the first runner-up is minimal — sometimes fractions of seconds. In the business world, executives must make high-stake decisions at a much faster pace. Therefore, in any difficult situations where you must make decisions and take actions, the way you control and replace your thoughts about what is important to achieve your goal ultimately drives your performance.

The key point to remember in any kind of mental training approach is that **you can do it only in the present moment.** You can't control your mind in the past; nor can you redirect it in the future. It is only the present moment where you can direct your mind to shift its thinking, and that will be responsible for any action you take.

Therefore, you need to consciously observe your thoughts from moment to moment and check the quality of those thoughts: Are they helping you to reach your goal or not? Continuously redirect and refocus your mind on resourceful thoughts; it will not be easy. If this were so, everyone would already be a high performer. Most people aren't even aware that they are getting swayed by endless thoughts, so the idea of replacing those thoughts is a foreign concept to them.

But if you are sincere enough to excel in their performance and design their life, this mental shift of consistent thought replacement, with some practice, can become your second nature and significantly upgrade the quality of your actions.

Master the Moments Between Stimulus and Response

In a thought-replacement technique, you primarily deal with your mind; you regulate the way it thinks and replace negative thoughts with resourceful ones that keep you focused on your goals.

But here is the thing: You don't get distracting or negative thoughts solely from your mind. Every day, you also have to deal with outside stimuli that trigger your emotions and motivate you to behave in a particular way. Another individual, or circumstances outside that you don't have direct control over, can disturb your mental state. You must choose an optimal response for that stimulus that doesn't adversely affect your performance.

In your inner battle, you must control your mind and regulate your ongoing thoughts moment-to-moment. However, while handling outside triggers, most people tend to abruptly respond; they are mostly influenced by their impulses, rather than any rational and thoughtful approach, which can have far-reaching adverse ramifications.

Most people don't realize that there is always a moment between the stimulus and response — a tiny space between when the stimulus hits you and you respond. You need to master that subtle moment. You need to train your mind to listen to your deep voice inside you that suggests the right response: the one which will best serve you.

For instance, in sports like soccer, sometimes a player intentionally pushes another person to the side in violation of the rules. Here, the innocent player, who gets hurt or distracted, has got a stimulus to immediately react, and he could choose either of the two options. He could follow his impulse, and in the spur of the moment, he might hurt the defaulting player in return. But this action could harm him, as both players could get a warning from the referee for violating the rules.

However, another thoughtful reaction to this stimulus is to let the referee intervene or to give an appropriate punishment or warning to the defaulting player; this will help the innocent player to focus his thoughts and play the game with a true sportsman spirit.

In this case, the stimulus is triggered by something external to you, and this gives you much less time to react; you are more prone to be guided by your impulses. Bring your awareness to that very tiny and subtle space; thoughtfully examine your alternatives and select an appropriate response. Once you find yourself aware of that space between stimulus and response, replace your negative thoughts with some resourceful thinking to find the best solution for you.

Let's take a real-life example:

Assume that you are driving on a busy road, and you have a fender-bender, which results in some scratches on your vehicle. Now this collision is a stimulus from outside that will trigger some response. But as you know now, there is always some space between stimulus and response. There could be two alternatives, as you might have rightly guessed.

One — that most often people do — is get out of the car and start shouting and blaming the other individual for this fender-bender. What might happen next is that you get entangled in a fight and spoil your mood – one that could ruin your entire day.

Select another alternative: Instead of reacting immediately, pause, park your car on the side and reach out to the other person. You already know whether this tiny accident was entirely the other person's fault or if you also had some role in it. But whatever the case, your car is already damaged. Now consider all possible options to handle the situation.

If you think that it was entirely the other person's fault, then simply ask him/her to compensate you for the damage. If the other person is considerate, he will admit that the accident was his fault and pay you the damages — matter solved.

Another scenario could be that he/she doesn't admit that the accident is his/her fault. Now think about how much the damage has been done to your vehicle. Does it make sense to call the traffic police and lodge a complaint, etc. — or just move on? Here is what will be the deciding factor. If you were heading towards an important meeting, and the damage is minimal, the whispering sound arising through awareness of that subtle space between this stimulus and response might guide you to ignore this small issue and continue on towards your meeting.

Neurologist Viktor Frankl, in his wonderful book *Man's Search for Meaning,* stated:

> *'Between stimulus and response, there is a space. In that space is our power to choose our response. In our response lies our growth and our freedom.'*

The more we can practice responding to any stimulus by enhancing our awareness of the short moment between stimulus and response, the better our choices will be in such moments.

Therefore, sustainable performance at higher levels for a longer period requires the consistent observation and training of your mind. The above mental shifts of thought replacements and enhancing your awareness before reacting to any stimulus can be developed by practicing mindfulness in your daily routine. Later in this book, you will understand the many benefits of mindfulness on your overall brain and body performance and how you can get started with mindfulness practice.

Avoid Mind Pollution to Strengthen Mental Muscles

Whatever our conscious minds get exposed, what we hear and see, gets stored in our subconscious mind. And later, whenever needed, our subconscious mind retrieves the relevant information from its memory bank and influences your behavior and actions. For example, if you always expose yourself to information that generates fear, scarcity, or any other kind of negative emotions, you increase the negativity in your subconscious mind.

To perform at your best, your mind needs to be energetic, focused, and distraction-free. Therefore, it is very important to safeguard our brain's cognitive powers and ensure that it doesn't get exposed to negativity or non-resourceful thoughts. Let's look at a few precautions which will help you to safeguard your mental faculties and keep them sharp and focused:

a. Be Smart With Your Smartphone

Your smartphone is probably the one technological invention that almost stays with you more than your shadow. This smart device has such an addictive power, the severity of which is probably equivalent — if not more — to smoking cigarettes or drinking alcohol. Your smartphone consumes your significant attention and willpower, and it exhausts your cognitive abilities if not used properly.

It is too difficult to resist the temptation to check your phone when it is near you. Such resistance to avoid looking at your phone consumes a lot of your mental energy. Instead of devoting your cognitive energy to what you are truly trying to accomplish, your attention mechanism gets distracted, wondering whether to respond to the notification that has just beeped on your phone. ==The more you try to resist checking your phone, the more it consumes your willpower and affects the quality of your focus in your important work.==

In a study published in *The Journal of Social Psychology*, researchers asked a group of college students to complete a series of difficult motor tasks when their cell phones were visible. Sure enough, their performance was significantly worse than a controlled group where participants' cell phones were not visible.

Surprisingly, things got even more interesting when all the participants' cell phones were removed, but the study leader's cell phone remained present in the room. Surprisingly, even when the phone visible wasn't their own, the participants' performance suffered.

You see how merely the visibility of a smartphone, even if it is not yours, can disturb your performance at work. You can estimate how consistent beeps and pop-up notifications on your smartphone distract you, worsening your performance.

There is evidence now that smartphone and their apps are designed in such a way that they do the job of making you addicted to these technologies. One of the renowned technology company's ex-product managers did a candid revelation in an interview[7], stating that the objective of the technology and online app-making companies is to hook the attention of the users. He compared the smartphone and the apps installed therein to a slot machine, where if someone starts looking, the machine hooks him/her by giving some instant rewards, such as new messages, likes, or follows, etc. According to

---

[7] https://vimeo.com/212594078

him, the objective of any smartphone app is not mainly to give the advantage to people in the form of information; rather, it is to make them feel that the smartphone and the apps are indispensable.

There is a psychology behind this known as the ***theory of unexpected reward***. Every time you look at your smartphone, you would see notifications, news or alerts. You'd have already noticed that, even before you have finished reading a post or news article, the app shows you the related stories that you might be interested in based on your viewing history or interests communicated because that's the way these for-profit companies can grab attention and sell you their product and services and display advertisements to make money from others. The ex-product manager compared this approach to reaching and capturing an individual's brainstem.

Therefore, for any high-performance enthusiast, the use of a smartphone must be minimal; it should be need-based, and after it is used it should be kept far from reach. At times, I keep my smartphone on just to take phone calls but deactivate the internet options. Through this approach, I can focus better on my creative work, i.e. writing books and other projects and enhance my performance. Once I am done with my quality work, then I put the phone on and check the notifications, alerts, etc., and generally, I find I have not missed anything major during those hours. However, I understand that everyone has his own circumstances or unique situations, and so their use of a smartphone, therefore, must vary accordingly. However, the basic idea is to use the smartphone to become *smarter* — not *addicted*.

Depending upon your role and responsibility in your organization, or if you work on your own, you should minimize the use of a smartphone as much as you can. Unless your job requires you to consistently be on your toes and use the internet uninterruptedly, you can disconnect from the virtual world and decide your preferred frequency of checking your notifications, etc. This will help you to significantly improve your attention and lead to high performance.

b. Turn Off the TV

The television, since its invention, has become one of the primary means by which most people relax and recover. If only watched — in moderation — for relaxation or with a specific objective of upgrading your knowledge, TV can entertain and educate you.

But for most people, watching television is the mental and emotional equivalent of eating junk food. You may feel a temporary form of recovery by watching television, but it is rarely nutritious, and it is easy to consume too much. Again, like smartphones, TV is another addiction tool to serve you commercials and advertisements that make you reach for your wallet to buy the advertiser's products.

Renowned researcher on the role of flow in high performance, Mihaly Csikszentmihalyi (you'll learn more about the flow in the later sections of this book), found that prolonged television watching is correlated with increased anxiety and low-level depression.

There are better recreational alternatives. Why not go for a walk with your loved ones in the evening instead of hitting the couch? Reading a great book, doing yoga or some meditation, and playing with your kids are all healthy and nutritious food for your brain. These activities will help you feel more joyful than watching a thriller or drama, which will leave you more exhausted after sitting for long hours.

To conclude, while it is very significant to make mental shifts to build your resilience and to ensure better performance, you need to be mindful that your reservoirs aren't simultaneously depleted by the excessive use of addictive technology.

You need to make sure that the bucket of your brain is not getting drained by the holes of addictions — only then can you store reserves of wisdom to use towards performing at your best levels.

With that, let's move on to the next section, where you will learn how to learn and master any skill needed to progress faster in your domain and, therefore, take your performance to the next level.

Chapter 3: Key Takeaways

Taking action at the highest level is largely a mental game; it requires you to make certain mental shifts, so that you start to think differently and, therefore, perceive situations differently before taking any actions. The key mental shifts are:

- **Take stress as a challenge, not as a threat.**

There are two kinds of stress. One that most people consider in the negative sense is distress, which is non-resourceful; however, there is a resourceful kind of stress known as "Eustress" — good stress that prepares you to accept the situation and rise to the challenge to achieve your goals.

Merely perceiving stress differently affects your neurochemistry. If you consider any kind of stress to be a threat, it releases a hormone called 'cortisol', which puts you into a fearful mode. But merely by perceiving stress as a challenge, you get a dose of DHEA, a neurosteroid that puts you into action mode to face the situation positively.

Dale Carnegie's offers his **formula to beat 90% of the stress in just four simple steps** as per below:

1. *Writing down precisely what I am worried about.*
2. *Writing down what I can do about it.*
3. *Deciding what to do.*
4. *Starting immediately to carry out that decision.*

- **Use consistent thought replacement from moment to moment.**

The idea behind consistent thought replacement is **to observe your thoughts from moment to moment and direct them towards your desired goal**; don't let your mind wander with some negative thoughts or criticism or mere distractions.

- **Master the moments between stimulus and response.**

Viktor Frankl, stated, *"Between stimulus and response there is a space. In that space is our power to choose our response. In our response lies our growth and our freedom."*

Instead of acting on our impulses and reacting immediately, we must realize that there is always some space between the stimulus that triggered our emotions and the way that we respond to that. If we master the tiny spaces between stimulus and response and choose the right actions, it will significantly enhance the quality of our lives.

- **Safeguard yourself from mind pollution from technological gadgets.**

Most of us, in our waking hours, are almost always surrounded by people, various forms of technology, and gadgets. Somehow, we still can manage to get away from other people after finishing our work-related duties, but technology and modern-day gadgets like smartphones and television are difficult to escape from.

For the most part, technological gadgets are made by for-profit companies to make people addicted to the screens so that they can sell their own products/servies or others' advertisements, as indicated by experts who have worked for such companies.

Performing at higher levels requires focus and undivided attention on the difficult goals for a longer time, so you can get into a state of flow, and, therefore, any distractions that can disturb your mind with non-resourceful information or cheap entertainment must be avoided.

Therefore, be smart with your smartphone, and turn off the television.

Chapter 4: How to Acquire and Upgrade Skills Effectively

****

"Acquire knowledge. Acquire skills. They weigh nothing, and you can carry them with you all your life."

~ Ruskin Bond"

To consistently perform at your highest level, you need to continuously adapt to ever-dynamic environments and learn new skills. Continuously learning and mastering new skills for your career empowers you to tap your full potential by using effective ways to perform and deliver results faster.

You are now aware of the concepts of homeostasis and neuroplasticity, by which you can reach any level of growth — barring a few genetic limitations. Your body can adapt to stressful situations through sufficient practice. Your mind is malleable and can change itself, regardless of age or any other fact, through exposure to new environments and behaviors. These concepts assure you that if you sincerely desire, you can become an altogether different person, regardless of location, religion, color, caste, gender — and you can reach any heights, as you have always wanted.

I've already put enough emphasis on the power of these principles to create human transformation by busting any myths or false beliefs about the limits people put on their capability to learn and grow.

With that now let's come to the nuts and bolts of how to learn and master skills. In this section, we will talk about a few strategies or techniques that will help you to learn new skills at a faster pace and without getting burned out.

Now let's look at these strategies:

The Principle of Stress and Recovery

Muhammad Ali, a famous boxer, once said, *"I don't count my sit-ups; I only start counting when it starts hurting because they're the only ones that count."*

Also the famous saying like this, *"No pain, no gain"*

You must stress yourself out and stretch your limits if you want to grow in any domain. If you dream of enjoying yourself at beaches with your solid six-pack or generally want a fit and active body, you know it takes work. You must expose your muscles to stress beyond their capacity — and only then do they grow. This principle applies everywhere; if you want to acquire any mental skill, you must stretch your mind beyond its normal capacity.

But here is the thing:

You can't continuously expose yourself to stress every time; otherwise, you'll face burnout, and that will backfire and ruin all the efforts you have invested so far.

To develop new skills, exposing yourself to stress is only half of the equation. The other important part of this principle is recovery.

The principles of stress and recovery apply to sports and every other area of life – to grow, you must implement a fair combination of stress and recovery periods; you must first stress your body and then give yourself the requisite rest. Therefore, the ultimate equation for growth without burnout is:

Stress + Recovery = Growth

Jim Loehr, a performance psychologist, in his book called *Toughness Training for Life,* describes the above formula below:

"It's important to understand that only rarely does the volume of stress defeat us; far more often, the agent of defeat is insufficient capacity for recovery after the stress. Great stress simply requires great recovery. **Your goal in toughness, therefore, is to be able to spike powerful waves of stress, followed by equally powerful troughs of recovery.** *So here is an essential Toughness Training Principle:* <u>Work hard. Recover equally hard.</u>

From a training perspective then, training recovery should receive as much attention as training stress. Unfortunately, that is rarely the case."

He offers the rule: *"Stress is the stimulus for growth. Recovery is when you grow."*

How Much Stress and How Much Recovery?

One important question that needs to be addressed in the stress and recovery principle is how much you should expose yourself to stress to grow instead of getting burned out.

The simple answer is to just take manageable challenges. Follow the Goldilocks principle: something should feel **just right**: not too easy, but not too hard – it should be just manageable. We should be stretching but not snapping; we are at the threshold where growth occurs without injury.

You should feel stress beyond your current capacity, but, at the same time, you should not end up injuring yourself. If you become injured, that will demoralize you – moreover, if you are hurt, you will have no choice but to take a break, and that will defeat the purpose as it will break the momentum of your training.

For example, let's assume that you have never run long distances and now, you want to give yourself the challenge of running a marathon. In almost all cases, if you think of the daunting task of suddenly running *twenty-six* miles, it will make you nervous if you have never run even a mile and have no idea about the training or structure for planning such long runs.

I went through this phase – though it was not a full marathon, but a shorter distance race. I had been thinking of participating in a half marathon for years, but it always seemed to me to be beyond my capacity or stamina and too hard to handle. Note that simply being aware of the principles of homeostasis doesn't help; you need to follow some effective strategies to affect that change. The first and foremost aspect of any strategy is to take up something challenging but not too much beyond your existing level of competency; it should be a challenge but something that you can manage to start with.

Let me share how I mastered the skill of running. First, I scoured the internet for training guides. I could find a few easily, thanks to Google. These guides told me to start slowly and gradually increase the stress level, i.e. distance, of running. Moreover, I learned that once I started doing half a mile on the first day, I couldn't keep on increasing every day. The training told me that I had first to build my capacity and stamina for running a particular distance for a few days – and then increase the distance by half a mile as a next step. Also, I was not supposed to run every day; rather, I was required to do some other exercises on alternate days, like cross-fit or some aerobic exercise, to stretch my whole body and give my legs and feet muscles a rest. With that approach, I was able to run up to *six* kilometers in a period of *eight* weeks – and in a period of *twelve* weeks, I was running up to *ten* kilometers. Then I participated in my first six-kilometer race in one half marathon event.

I know it is not that big an achievement, and, therefore, I can't brag about it. The idea was to honestly share my own experience of researching – and then applying – the principle of stress and recovery in learning the skill of long-distance running. I was not aware at that time about this principle; however, in hindsight, I realized that the stress levels needed and the duration of recovery were very professionally structured in the training I underwent.

Is there a magic number by which one should stretch?

To some people, following the Goldilocks principle – i.e. assessing what is 'just right' – may not give the precise idea or guidance. Thankfully, some research was conducted by Steve Kotler, the author of the book: *The Rise of Superman*, where he tells us about the magic stretch number being ***four percent* beyond your existing capacity**. He says:

*"This is why the challenge/skills ratio is so important. **If we want to achieve the kinds of accelerated performance we're seeing in action and adventure sports, then it's 4 percent plus 4 percent plus 4 percent, day after day, week after week, months into years into careers**. This is the road to real magic. Follow this path long enough, and not only does impossible becomes possible, but it also becomes what's next—like eating breakfast or another day at the office."*

To me, a ***four percent increase at a time seems just something right and not that hard***. It is like, if you can do twenty-five pushups in a day, then your stretch would be *just adding one more push-up the next time you do it."*

Finally, when the principle of just-manageable stress (with recovery) is combined with the principle of compound effect (that comes from daily practice), the real magic starts to happen. If seen across a longer timeframe, daily small progress at incremental levels would surprise you. In fact, you would look at your results and wonder at what you have become and how far you had come with your consistent progress with just manageable stretches.

As a writer, I know that if one consistently writes between 1,500-2,000 words in a day, then it will take him or her up to three to four weeks (with some rest days included) to see the first draft of a manuscript of a reasonably sized book. Writing a specific number of words per day is a stretch for anyone starting out, but it is still manageable compared to writing a book in one stretch. Small chunks of work – done regularly – don't burn you out, and it takes care of the recovery part as well.

Therefore, use the principles of stress and recovery for real growth because continuous stress and no recovery will lead only to burnout. On the other hand, very little or no stress will not cause you to grow much. Follow the Goldilocks principle. Take on manageable challenges. Get the required rest after stress, and all this together consistently will lead you to acquire any skills in a reasonably short period.

How to Steal Rest – Even in High-Stake and Stressful Situations

The concepts of stress and recovery apply not only in voluntary attempts to gain muscles or acquire new skills, such as when we are in a low-stake environment. But it is also very well introduced by high performers, even when they are in a high-stake environment, when repercussions of any mistake are catastrophic.

It is, of course, difficult to fathom the idea of taking any long recovery break when you are amid real action. You could also debate that there is no luxury or scope of taking the smallest amount of rest or recovery when you are in a high-stake performance zone.

You might also argue that amid an argument in a high-stake litigation matter in court, a lawyer doesn't have the luxury of time to stop arguing the case, take a rest, think about it, and resume the argument after that – no, it can't happen that way.

But I have something surprising to tell you – even in tough and highly demanding situations when you can't imagine taking any rest, high performers develop the skill of stealing the briefest of recovery periods (a few seconds) –

and that changes the entire game. Let's look at a real-life example to support this point.

Jim Loehr and Tony Schwartz, in their book, *The Power of Full Engagement,* give an example of how the best tennis players are able to maintain their level of performance till the last sets of the game when they have exhausted a substantial portion of their physical energy and stamina.

You might be thinking that they have developed the stamina to sustain for longer periods through practice. But the close observation of these extreme players revealed the **subtle infusion of the element of rest** – even in the highly demanding and high-stake championship match of tennis.

Jim Loehr states that in his role as a performance psychologist, he had set a goal to understand the factors that set apart the greatest competitors in the world from the rest of the pack. He was working with world-class tennis players and had already spent hundreds of hours watching top players and studying tapes of their matches.

To his growing frustration, he could detect almost no significant differences in their competitive habits during the game points. It was only then that he noticed **what these high performers did between points that he suddenly saw a subtle difference.**

While most of them were not aware of it, the best players had each built a similar set of routines between points. These included the way they walked back to the baseline after a point, how they held their heads and shoulders, where they focused their eyes, the pattern of their breathing – and even the way they talked to themselves.

Loehr explains that **in those *sixteen to twenty* seconds between the points, the best tennis players were able to *lower their heart rates by as much as twenty beats per minute*.** The heart rates of their competitors who didn't have the same dialed-in rest rituals often stayed at the same levels.

From the above, it becomes very clear that the player who can squeeze in *twenty* seconds of rest after an intense game point – vis-à-vis his/her opponent, who is just pushing himself/herself hard and relying more on his/her stamina and willpower, will be in a better position to win the game. The players who learned the skill of grabbing mini recovery periods in those intense game points were able to generate additional does of energy, and, therefore, overpower their competitors, who were consistently depleting their energy after each game point.

Similarly, in the business world, when the financial or business stakes are high, when one has to make tough decisions and execute them, the key executives take deeper breaths to get calmer; this approach creates recovery periods and re-energizes them to deliver their best performances.

Travel Between the Learning and Performance Zones

As we all know, the only constant thing in life is change. Nothing is constant, and everything keeps changing. Even our body replaces itself with a largely new set of body cells every seven to ten years, and some of our most important parts are revamped even more rapidly, as research[8] has found. In other words, we become essentially new people every few years, without even realizing it – that's the pace of life changes.

Most people think they have developed enough skills and can handle complex tasks – and, therefore, they can relax without bothering to learn or upgrade their knowledge. But they miss out on the fact that the challenges of life and its complexities keep on adding up every day. Also, today's economy is knowledge-based, technology is improving every day, and the existing knowledge is rapidly becoming obsolete. Moreover, the competitors in your field continue

---

[8] https://science.howstuffworks.com/life/cellular-microscopic/does-body-really-replace-seven-years.htm

to learn and implement new knowledge or new products.

High performance is all performing consistently at higher levels and sustainably. You are already applying your current skill set and experience in your work or performance zone. But the problem is that if you just stay in your performance zone, relying solely on your existing skill set, the frequent changes in technology or the nature of your work will soon make your current skill set obsolete.

Therefore, to play the high-performance game – for a long haul and sustainably – you must consistently upgrade your learning while performing.

Let's put it this way: you must consistently travel between your performance and learning zones.

A learning zone is a period in our lives when we are focused on learning to improve our skills. Performance zones are the areas when we are just performing the skills we learn.

The learning zone is when our goal is to improve. Then we do activities designed for improvement, concentrating on what we haven't mastered yet, which means we must expect to make mistakes, knowing that we will learn from them. And this is entirely different from what we do in our performance zone.

In the **performance zone, our goal is to do something the best we can to execute it**. In this zone, we concentrate on what we have already mastered, and we try to minimize mistakes.

One of the key requirements for high performance that most highly effective people follow is to **continuously travel between the learning zone and the performance zone.** They go through life deliberately, alternating between two zones: the learning and the performance zones.

The problem with most people is that they think that after they are out of school or college and have earned their degrees or diplomas, the learning stops there – they think that learning is over.

In his wonderful talk[9], Eduardo Briceño, from Mindset Works, a growth mindset training company, explains how we can improve at the things we do care about.

He cites the example of Demosthenes, a political leader, great orator in ancient Greece, and a lawyer. To become a great orator and lawyer, Demosthenes didn't always remain in the

---

[9]
https://www.ted.com/talks/eduardo_briceno_how_to_get_better_at_the_things_you_care_about

performance zone. Rather, he spent time learning the skills. He studied for long hours about law and philosophy. But he also heard many great speeches to learn and master his public speaking skills. He had a lisp problem (a minor speech defect), so to speak clearly, he put stones in his mouth and then practiced speaking. Such practice, with greater emphasis on learning correctly and improve yourself by feedback, is known as deliberate practice (we will cover in detail in later sections of the book).

If you carefully observe successful people around the world, the more successful they are, the more time they spend in the learning zone; they simply don't remain in the performance zone.

Look at the practice sessions of Olympic gold medalists and other athletes – everyone spends an enormous amount of time earning and practicing their craft. You will find CEOs and top-notch corporate officials spending significant time in conferences, learning from other industry colleagues. They have clearly understood that if they simply remain in the performance zone, they will not get any new insights from the marketplace and become obsolete. They know it is the learning zone that will help them to improve their knowledge and skills that will prepare them for the next level of growth and enhance their competence to perform better.

I had been a corporate lawyer for many years and can confirm one thing based on my interaction with many legal eagles: they all travel between the learning and performance zones almost every day. Have you ever seen a litigation attorney's work schedule? They argue the cases in courts all day long, and in the evening, and sometimes for long nights, they research court judgments and precedents to prepare themselves for the litigation matters and schedule for the hearing the next morning. The same holds true with any other profession – they must all constantly upgrade themselves.

High performers know very well that staying in the performance zone keeps their performance at their current level. But immersing in the learning zone helps them to improve their future potential and achieve faster growth in their life.

Eduardo then gives another example of Beyoncé, an American singer and songwriter who also consistently travels between the learning and the performance zones. When she is performing a show in the evening, she is in the performance zone. But once the show is over, she then enters the learning zone. She is known to watch the videos of her shows in the evening and note the areas that could be improved for future shows. The next morning, her team of musicians, dancers, and other staff get pages of notes on what needs to be modified for the next show. Therefore, she is on the continuous journey between the learning and the performance zones.

How to Spend More Time in the Learning Zone

With all that, the next question that comes up is: how can we spend more time in the learning zone? There are a few ways to do that: the first and foremost condition is that we must believe that we can improve. That's what was referred to as a growth mindset by researcher Carol Dweck. Secondly, we all must have a desire to learn, as nothing changes until we truly desire to improve. Then, we need to create some low stake environments, where even if we do something wrong, there should not be any catastrophic outcomes. For example, a tightrope walker doesn't practice new tricks without a net underneath him/her, and an athlete wouldn't try a new move during a championship match.

Now the key problem is that our environments are always too high-stake, so we have no choice except to remain in our performance zones. Most of the corporate cultures promote flawless execution, and that's a good approach. But ideally, beneath this culture, there should be some scope of trying newer ways and experimenting with innovative ideas, knowing that the idea may go wrong, as trying and testing different ways is also the way to learn and improve in anything.

So, in such high-stake performance zones, what should be the approach for switching to a learning zone? Eduardo suggests that the solution is to create low-stake islands in the high- stake seas. It is through talking to our mentors or trusted colleagues, with whom we can talk about the things we don't know or that we need to improve upon. People should be given some time to learn newer techniques through education conferences or through attending seminars or conferences.

If someone can consistently shift the gears between the learning zone and the performance zone, they start to immensely improve the quality of their performance.

The next section of the book will build upon what you learnt in this chapter; it will teach you the best way to learn by a refined form of practice that is necessary to gain mastery and expertise in any skill.

Chapter 4: Key Takeaways

You can't perform at excellent levels – and, therefore, can't grow faster – if you don't focus on acquiring new skills or upgrade your existing skills to the next level.

But you don't want to spend ages learning or upgrading your skills, and you need some effective techniques to develop skills faster. Here are some key ways you can acquire any skills faster and sustainably:

- **The principle of stress and recovery for growth**

The formula for growth in any area of life is to expose yourself to stress but also ensure that you recover well. Here is the growth equation looks like:

Stress + Recovery = Growth

As rightly stated by performance psychologist Jim Loehr, "...***Stress is the stimulus for growth. Recovery is when you grow.***"

But don't overstretch yourself while stressing out – rather, take on manageable challenges. Use the Goldilocks principle, which means that something is 'just right'. We should be stretching but not snapping. We are at the threshold where growth occurs without injury.

Steve Kotler suggests the magic stretch number as four percent beyond your existing capacity. He says: *"**If we want to achieve the kinds of accelerated performance we're seeing*** *in action and adventure sports, then it's 4 percent plus 4 percent plus 4 percent, day after day, week after week, months into years into careers..."*

Also, try to introduce rest, even into high-stake environments or complex situations, by slowing down your breathing and relaxing; you'll be able to make better decisions.

- **Travel between the learning and performance zones.**

Learning doesn't end when you finish school or college, it's a life-long journey.

Even after you have started your career, don't just rely on merely getting experience in your performance zone. Instead, **you should often travel between the performance and learning zones to improve the quality of your work by implementing the new ways as you continuously learn**.

Chapter 5: Build Expertise and Attain Mastery in Anything You Do

****

"Mastery is not a function of genius or talent. It is a function of time and intense focus applied to a particular field of knowledge."

~ Robert Greene

You might have heard the age-old saying:

"Practice makes a man perfect."

But this is not entirely true.

You don't become an expert doctor solely by being a doctor for many years. You don't become a top accountant or a lawyer just by working in that capacity for years. Though experience – to some extent – plays a role in improvement, you can't simply become an expert in any field by learning through work experience only.

If spending a number of years in any particular field can make someone an expert, then all the elderly would be paid immensely and retire as multi-millionaires. But that's not true; someone could claim to have *twenty* years of experience in a particular field – but in reality, it could be one year of experience just repeated over *twenty* years without learning anything new.

Therefore, practicing the same things over and over without focusing on improving your craft doesn't make you an expert. Hence, the improved version of this quote should be:

"Perfect practice makes a man perfect".

You don't become an expert in something merely by practicing; rather, **expertise is earned by practicing it with the right set of knowledge**.

This section is all about teaching what should be the right way to practice and become an expert in your field, deliver excellent performance, and generate exceptional results.

Anders Ericsson, a psychologist and researcher at Florida State University, is known for his vast research into the subject of how people become the best in what they do. In fact, he was the original researcher of the famous 10,000-hour rule, which was promoted by Malcolm Gladwell in his famous book *Outliers,* as the period needed to become an expert in any field.

Ericsson explains that there are **three types of practices** people pursue to gain any skill in any field, as stated below:

a. Naive practice
b. Purposeful practice
c. Deliberate practice.

Let's look at each of these one by one and learn why Ericsson emphasizes that **only deliberate practice is the way to attaining the status of expert** or master of any particular field.

1. Naive practice means a generic kind of mindless practice, where you simply keep on doing what you have learned earlier. It's like always being in the performance zone and just taking actions solely based on your existing knowledge and skill set, without any focus or intention of improvement. This type of practice of doing the same thing repeatedly – and expecting that it will improve – doesn't work. Rather, this was termed as insanity by the famous Albert Einstein: *"The definition of insanity is doing the same thing over and over and expecting different results."*

It is like continuing to play guitar from college days until your *forties* without deliberately learning the best ways to press the right nodes and strings — and expecting that the *twenty* years of practice will make you a better guitarist.

You don't get the benefit of homeostasis and neuroplasticity by repeating the same thing mindlessly and repeatedly without any intention of learning to do it the right way.

To understand what best serves you in your drive to become an expert, let's first look at the other two types of practices.

2. **Purposeful Practice**: This is a much better way to practice and learn a skill faster, as compared to naive practice. Here are the **features of purposeful practice**:

    a. Purposeful practice has **well-defined and specific goals**. Take the example of any sports training or learning any new language or playing any musical instrument within a particular time frame. Here you have a clear objective to learn a skill in a particular time frame.
    b. Purposeful practice is **focused**. This kind of practice is not like a casual visit to a grocery store, mindlessly wandering and grabbing anything you like. You need to be entirely focused on the skill that you want to learn. If you are allowing anything to disturb you in that activity, that's not a

focused practice – you will end up just wasting your time – and not learning anything significant that can deliver measurable results.

c. Purposeful practice **requires feedback**. You need to know how you're practicing at different stages of your practice. Did you miss a note playing that song you wanted to play perfectly during your guitar practice? <u>Immediate feedback to help you identify what you're doing wrong</u> (and how you can improve) is essential.

d. Purposeful practice requires you to **get out of your comfort zone**; this is one of the most important elements of purposeful practice. If you don't push yourself beyond your comfort zone, you will never improve.

Anyone can realize that practicing with well-defined and specific goals, in a focused manner, with an appropriate feedback system about your mistakes, and consistently pushing yourself beyond the comfort zone – contains all the necessary elements to learn any new skills and stimulate improvement. That's why purposeful practice is certainly a great way to learn anything new.

Purposeful practice appears to be great, and it is the only way to go – unless you know about the third type of practice told by Ericsson, known as deliberate practice. Let's examine this now.

3. **Deliberate Practice:** That's the gold standard of any practice; this practice has all the elements of the purposeful practice, but, **additionally, it has the added element of coaching or teaching through a clear training program** in the established field.

Deliberate practice involves the pursuit of learning or upgrading any skills via well-defined, specific goals, with focused areas of expertise, improving upon on your mistakes regularly and pushing yourself beyond your comfort zone all the time, as required in purposeful practice, but it also **requires a teacher or coach who has demonstrated an ability to help others improve the desired area of expertise**—say chess, tennis, or music—and who can provide continuous feedback.

Think about Tiger Woods, the titan of the golf. Do you think he needs any training or coaching to play golf? He hired a swing coach for long periods of time to correct his swing. He knows very well that only owning an expensive club set couldn't make him win the game – it is the mastery of his craft that will help him to remain at the top of his game. He understands the importance of deliberate practice under expert guidance to consistently improve and master his game.

Ericsson states that **just working harder or working more does not seem to be associated with high levels of performance**. Rather, if you're working with a teacher or a mentor who has attained a high level of performance, that individual can help you to design the kind of training activities that they may have engaged in to reach that higher level of performance.

He states: *"It's not just a matter of accumulating hours. If you're doing your job, and you're just doing more and more of the same, you're not actually going to get better."*

Here, I have cited[10] an illustration of normal practice versus deliberate practice to help you to better understand their differences.

Normal Practice

- Start with a general idea of what the child wants to do (play tennis).
- Find a tennis group or lessons; play with parents, siblings, friends.

---

[10] https://qz.com/915646/how-to-make-your-kid-good-at-anything-according-to-anders-ericsson-an-expert-on-peak-performance-and-originator-of-the-10000-hour-rule/

- Practice until the child reaches an acceptable level.
- Get a coach.
- Play more.
- Continue improving.

Deliberate practice

- Start with a general idea of what the child wants to do (play tennis).
- Find a tennis group or lessons; play with parents, siblings, friends.
- Practice until the child reaches an acceptable level.
- Get a coach who can **set specific targets** and tailor practice to improve those areas (e.g. improve forehand).
- Develop a **way to measure improvement**; if forehands are a weakness, the coach delivers lots of those strokes, progressively makes them harder to return, and demands that the player places strokes in a specific spot. **Their progress is tracked constantly**.
- Create **positive channels for feedback** so that modifications are continuous (like learning how not to reveal one's intentions to one's opponent).
- Develop a **mental representation of excellent performance**: what to do in various game situations, how to respond

to certain shots, and when to take risks and try new things.
- Coach designs **developmentally-appropriate training sessions** to achieve maximum effort and concentration.
- A kid **learns to self-assess and come up with his/her own mental representations** so they feel in charge and able to exploit opportunities on the court.
- A kid **develops own training sessions to elicit maximum effort and concentration**, acknowledging physical and mental limits and learns to use self-assessment to address weaknesses.

That's why experts appear to be so effortless in what they do – their underlying deliberate practice has already created strong mental representations in their minds that help them make quick decisions in complex situations. Ericsson succinctly explains below how the inner brain structure and neural circuit changes with deliberate practice:

"The main thing that sets experts apart from the rest of us is that **their years of practice have changed the neural circuitry in their brains to produce highly specialized mental representations**, which, in turn, make possible the incredible **memory, pattern**

recognition, problem-solving, and other sorts of advanced abilities needed to excel in their particular specialties. The **more you study a subject, the more detailed your mental representations of it become**, and the better you get at assimilating new information."

I loved his wonderful thoughts when he says:

"There is no reason not to follow your dream. Deliberate practice can open the door to a world of possibilities that you may have been convinced were out of reach. Open that door."

The above statement is an assurance to achieve anything you want to achieve in your life, and the tools of deliberate practice will make it possible for you to fulfill your dreams.

Chapter 5: Key Takeaways

Mere practice doesn't make your perfect; rather, you must practice with the right set of knowledge and tools to attain expertise and become a master in your chosen domain.

Anders Ericsson, a researcher and psychologist at Florida State University, explained there are **three types of practices** people pursue to gain any skill in any field, as stated below:

- **Naive practice**

Naive practice is a **generic kind of mindless practice**, where you simply keep on doing what you have already learned.

This is the case where *twenty* years of experience in a particular field is nothing but one year of experience just repeated over *twenty* years without learning anything new.

- **Purposeful practice** has the following features.

    a. **Well-defined and specific goals**.
    b. Purposeful practice is **<u>focused</u>**.
    c. Purposeful practice **requires feedback**.
    d. Purposeful practice **gets out of your comfort zone**.

- **Deliberate practice.**

This practice has all the elements of the purposeful practice – but, **additionally, it has the element of coaching or teaching added to it through a clear training program** in the established field.

Deliberate practice changes internal brain structure

Deliberate practice for a number of years **changes the neural circuitry of the practitioner's brains to produce highly specialized mental representations**, which, in turn, make possible the incredible **memory, pattern recognition, problem-solving, and other advanced abilities** needed to excel in their particular specialties.

Chapter 6: Science-Backed Ways to Boost Willpower for Focused Performance

****

"Strength does not come from physical capacity. It comes from an indomitable will."

~ Mahatma Gandhi

In the previous sections, we learned that it's only with deliberate practice that one can achieve mastery in any field.

This deliberate practice towards attaining mastery and taking consistent and massive actions towards your most important goals requires you to build deep focus and resist distractions like social media notification beeps or the other people around you.

Of course, clarity about your most important goals gives you the necessary pull to stay on track, but the world around you doesn't care about your goals – everyone out there has their own agenda and priorities. It is critical to develop the willpower to stay focused on your goals and not get distracted by any outside stimuli or disturbance. Willpower is also required to tame your emotions at times when strong impulses tend to overpower you.

Therefore, willpower is one of the most important ingredients of the recipe of high performance.

For example, I'm writing this chapter with full clarity about my goal of serving my readers with the noble objective of improving their performance. However, at times I feel the urge to check my WhatsApp messages (which I always keep on silent mode) or statistics on my laptop. Here comes the role of willpower to guard myself against any distractions from technology or people around me.

Think of willpower like putting blinders on each side of a horse's eyes, so that horse can focus only on the front and applies all its energy to running faster.

Roy Baumeister, a psychologist at Florida State University, describes[11] **three necessary components for achieving any of your goals**. First, you need to establish the motivation for change and set a clear goal. Second, you need to monitor your behavior toward that goal. The third component is willpower. Whether your goal is to lose weight, kick a smoking habit, study more, or spend less

---

[11] http://www.apa.org/helpcenter/willpower.aspx

time on Facebook, willpower is a critical step to achieving that outcome.

What exactly is willpower?

Willpower is our **ability to control and resist our short-term temptations to enable us to achieve our longer-term goals**. It is also known as determination, self-control, or self-discipline.

Willpower is the force that can keep us glued to the actions that are essential to achieve our long-term goals. As achieving goals take a considerable amount of time, our internal desires to enjoy instant gratification often cause us to drift from our path, and that's where willpower will help us to deliver the highest level of performance.

In this section, we will talk about how one can develop willpower that enables one to take massive actions towards achieving our goals. Let's look at some of the best ways to improve your willpower.

- **Practice Daily Meditation**

Whether you live in the East or West, meditation is not only a religious or spiritual activity. As confirmed by science, meditation offers benefits to our general well-being and improved functionality in all facets of life.

It is no longer considered a mystical eastern ritual. Many high-achievers and successful people have already incorporated a meditation practice into their routine to increase their daily productivity.

Tim Ferriss, a best-selling author, has also interviewed hundreds of hugely successful people from diverse backgrounds, including business tycoons, top sports athletes, and the best creative minds around the world, such as Arnold Schwarzenegger, Jamie Foxx, Edward Norton, Tony Robbins, Maria Sharapova, Peter Thiel, Amanda Palmer, Malcolm Gladwell, and many more.

He categorically states that one of the most common rituals or daily practices followed by more than 80% of these interviewees is that they have adopted some form of meditation or mindfulness practice in their daily routine – a consistent pattern of a secluded practice to be with themselves.

Ferriss, who himself is a successful author, entrepreneur, and investor, states the benefits as follows: "Through 20 minutes of consistent meditation, I can become a commander, looking out at the battlefield from a hilltop. I'm able to look at a map

of the territory and make high-level decisions."

What Is Meditation?

Meditation is a process of traveling inside yourself – throughout your body and mind – by noticing everything happening inside you at any given moment and enhancing your awareness about the ongoing thoughts and emotions within you.

Psychologist and researcher Kelly McGonigal, in her wonderful book, *The Willpower Instinct*, describes the benefits of meditation on the willpower:

*"Neuroscientists have now found that when we make ourselves sit and instruct our brain to meditate, not does it gets better at meditating, but **it develops a wide range of self-control skills, including attention, focus, stress management, impulse control, and self-awareness**. Science tells us that people who meditate regularly for longer periods have **more gray matter** in their prefrontal cortexes, as well as in other regions of the brain that support self-awareness."*

She further explains that you don't need a lifetime of meditation to see results; an intense meditation – for only a few hours – provides great benefits. She states:

*"Some researchers have started to look for the smallest dose of meditation needed to see benefits. One study found that just **three hours of meditation practice led to improved attention and self-control**. After eleven hours, researchers could see those changes in the brain.*

The new meditators had increased neural connections between regions of the brain important for staying focused, ignoring distractions, and controlling impulses. *Another study found that eight weeks of daily meditation practice led to increased self-awareness in everyday life, as well as increased gray matter in corresponding areas of the brain. It may seem incredible that our brains can reshape themselves so quickly, but **meditation increases blood flow to the prefrontal cortex in much the same way that lifting weights increases blood flow to your muscles.** The brain appears to adapt to exercise in the same way that muscles do, getting both bigger and faster to get better at what you ask of it."*

I've been meditating for quite a few years now, but not very regularly. However, over the last few months, I do it every morning and in the evening before going to bed. I am starting to sense thoughts, emotions, and even tiny vibrations in my body. I am starting to make a fine distinction between different thoughts and emotions in my mind and body.

The most important benefit is that I often find myself able to rid my mind of my negative emotions or desires for instant gratification — and simultaneously, I can ask my mind to focus on resourceful thoughts that will lead me towards accomplishing my goals. I can honestly tell you that it is an amazing feeling when you can control yourself and focus only on your next steps. Furthermore, once you start meditating and start enjoying the benefits of it, then you won't feel like skipping it — even for a single day.

How to Practice Mindfulness Daily

You don't need hours to get started with mindfulness. You can start with just ten minutes every morning and gradually increase to twenty minutes a day — enough to help you disengage from your thoughts and look at the world with a renewed perspective.

Mindfulness meditation expert Sam Harris compares meditation to walking on a tightrope: it's easy to explain but

difficult to master. He goes on to describe the steps necessary for a proper mindfulness practice[12].

1. Sit comfortably with your spine erect, either in a chair or cross-legged on a cushion.

2. Close your eyes, take a few deep breaths and feel the points of contact between your body and the chair or floor. Notice the sensations associated with sitting — feelings of pressure, warmth, tingling, vibration, etc.

3. Gradually become aware of the process of breathing. Pay attention to wherever you feel your breath most clearly — either in your nostrils or in the rising and falling of your abdomen.

---

[12] https://www.samharris.org/blog/item/how-to-meditate

4. Allow your attention to rest in the mere sensation of breathing. (There is no need to control your breath; let it come and go naturally.)

5. Every time your mind wanders, gently return it to the sensation of breathing.

6. As you focus on your breath, you will notice that other perceptions and sensations continue to appear: sounds, feelings in the body, emotions, etc. Simply notice these phenomena as they emerge in your field of awareness, and then return to the sensation of breathing.

7. The moment you observe that you are lost in thought, notice the present thought as an object of consciousness. Then return

your attention to the breath — or to whatever sounds or sensations arise in the next moment.

8. Continue in this way until you witness all sights, sounds, sensations, emotions — and even thoughts themselves — as they arise and pass away.

Those who are new to the practice generally find it useful to hear instructions spoken aloud in the form of guided meditation.

There are plenty of apps available these days to help you to do a guided meditation:

One meditation mobile app I have tried is called *Headspace*. It is a guided form of meditation that helps you scan through your thoughts, see your thoughts clearly, and get into a state of total relaxation. You can find in an Android version, as well as an iOS one, at the following link: https://www.headspace.com

Another recommended guided meditation app is

called *Welzen*, and you may check it out at https://welzen.org/

Breathe More Slowly to Beat Stress

You will be amazed to know how one simple technique of slowing down the pace of your breathing helps to improve your willpower.

Here is what you need to do under this stress-busting technique.

Breathe slowly – so slowly that you take just four to six breaths per minute. Each breath in and out will take ten to fifteen seconds.

To measure and ensure that you are doing it properly, breathe in slowly for a count of four, and breathe out for a count of six. Do this a few times, and you will feel a sense of relief from your anxiety; instead, you'll find yourself getting clarity about taking the next action towards your goals.

Explaining the benefit of this technique of slow breathing, Kelly McGonigal states that the **slowdown of breathing activates the prefrontal cortex and increases heart rate variability, which helps shift the brain and body from a state of stress to self-control mode.** A few minutes of this technique will make you feel calm, in control, and capable of handling cravings or challenges

Remember, you don't need to hold your breath. It will increase your stress. One important thing to remember is that you should focus more on exhaling, rather than inhaling. Once you pay more attention to emptying your body of air, it will automatically breathe in.

Now let's move on to the next technique for developing willpower.

Exercise is the Wonder Drug for Willpower

Albert Einstein once said, *"Nothing happens until something moves."*

That applies to our bodies, too; we must move our bodies to improve the health of our internal organs by increasing our blood circulation, which gives us the energy to perform at our best levels. Again, Kelly McGonigal describes the benefits of exercise as a wonder drug to develop your willpower. She states:

"Exercise turns out to be the closest thing to a wonder drug for self-control that scientists have discovered. For starters, the willpower benefits of exercise are immediate. **Fifteen minutes on a treadmill reduces cravings***, as seen when researchers try to tempt dieters with chocolate and smokers with cigarettes. The long-term effects of exercise are even more impressive.* **It not only relieves ordinary, everyday stress, but it's as powerful an antidepressant as Prozac.** *Working out also*

enhances the biology of self-control by increasing baseline heart rate variability and training the brain. When neuroscientists have peered inside the brains of new exercisers, they have seen **increases in both gray matter (brain cells) and white matter, the insulation on brain cells that helps them communicate quickly and efficiently with each other**. *Physical exercise—like meditation — makes your brain bigger and faster, and the prefrontal cortex shows the largest training effect."*

Therefore, incorporate some kind of exercise habits into your daily routine, such as running, cycling, swimming, hitting the gym, or enrolling in some outside sports like badminton, tennis or any other sports that require you to move your body with intensity for at least twenty to thirty minutes a day.

Use Self-Control Exercises to Build Your Willpower

Willpower is also like a muscle, and if you engage yourself in mini self-control exercises, they will help you to build your willpower over time. Activities like making your bed in the morning after you wake up, improving your sitting posture continuously, and cutting back on sweets, etc., play a role in improving your overall willpower.

Martha Beck, a sociologist life coach and author, once said, "*The way we do anything is the way we do everything*." **If you practice exercising self-control on small and inconsequential things, you will tend to improve your willpower in important areas of your life,** i.e. focusing on your work, taking care of your health and taming your emotions better.

How small self-control exercises help us to develop our willpower is explained by Heidi Grant Halvorson in her book, *Succeed*. She states:

*"If you want more self-control, you can get more. **And you get more self-control the same way you get bigger muscles — you've got to give it regular workouts**. Recent research has shown that engaging in daily activities, such as exercising, keeping track of your finances or what you are eating — or even just remembering to sit up straight every time you think of it — can help you develop your overall self-control capacity.*

For example, in one study, students who were assigned to (and stuck to) a daily exercise program not only got physically healthier, but they also became more likely to wash dishes instead of leaving them in the sink, and less likely to impulsively spend money."

One annual survey conducted by the American Psychological Association[13] about the level of stress in America asks, among other things, about participants' abilities to make healthy lifestyle changes. Survey participants regularly cite a lack of willpower as the top reason for not following through with implementing such lifestyle changes.

Fortunately, you don't need to spend a hefty amount of money, take any medication, or visit any medical specialists to address your lack of willpower. The solutions are easily available to anyone at home. It is only a matter of putting in a very little sum of willpower to start with the techniques stated above, and anyone can start seeing the results in terms of enhanced willpower. And the most important benefit you'll derive from these small self-control exercises will be that you'll improve your focus, which will allow you to work longer without getting swayed by distractions and, consequently, improve your performance.

Bring Precision and Specificity to the Timing of Your Actions

Willpower depletes through vague directions. **The more specific you are about the timing and action to be taken, the more**

---

[13] http://www.apa.org/helpcenter/willpower.aspx

likely that you will be able to use willpower to your advantage.

Some studies confirm that the specificity of timing and the precision of behavior significantly increase the likelihood of success. We don't get an infinite supply of willpower every day, and every small decision depletes the willpower.

Knowing this principle, many successful people plan their daily routines so that it doesn't take their willpower and time to make decisions. For example, every Sunday evening, they decide what clothes they will wear and what meals they will eat each day for the entire next week. The objective is to remove the day-to-day problems that absorb the most meaningful portion of your day.

Former United States President Barack Obama once said, "You'll see I wear only gray or blue suits; I'm trying to pare down decisions. **I don't want to make decisions about what I'm eating or wearing. Because I have too many other decisions to make.**" If we waste our energy by making too many small decisions, we'll have less energy to make the more critical ones.

Our pre-frontal cortex is responsible for executive decision-making and other important functions that require conscious thinking efforts. **By determining when, where, and how**

any behavior will occur, we no longer need to think about how to complete an activity done — and that way, we get things done faster.

In one interesting experiment, a group of drug addicts were studied during withdrawal — a period of abrupt discontinuation or decrease in the intake of medications or recreational drugs. During this period, the energy required to control the urge to consume the drug severely affected their ability to carry out any other task. During this withdrawal period, one group of addicts was asked to commit to writing a short resume **before a particular time on a particular day**; this was to help them find post-rehabilitation employment. Not even one succeeded. A second group was asked to complete the same task, but the group was additionally told **exactly when and where they would write the resume**. The result was that **eighty percent of people in the second group succeeded**.

It proves that the specificity of time and the precision of action to be taken safeguard the use of willpower. Therefore, next time, don't give yourself any vague instructions; rather, decide in advance the precise time and precise action to safeguard your willpower to get most out of your days.

Build Rituals to Safeguard Willpower

All highly effective people use well-crafted rituals to perform their tasks. Rituals can be defined as carefully determined and well-structured behavior that is purposefully incorporated into our daily routines.

Willpower requires pushing yourself to do a particular action; rituals pull you towards them. For example, taking a shower in the morning and brushing your teeth are daily rituals. You don't need to use any willpower or discipline yourself to undertake these morning routines — you don't ever feel a need to push yourself to do these activities.

Rituals ensure that we use as little of our cognitive capacity as possible during such activities because they get deeply rooted in our subconscious brain through enough practice, and then start to happen almost at a subconscious level without much of our active involvement. This spares a ton of willpower to strategically focus on our other most important pursuits.

All the performers rely on positive rituals to manage their energy and regulate their behavior. It is also said that the more exciting the challenge and the greater the pressure, the more rigorous our rituals need to be. Robin Sharma, in his study of the world's high performers, discovered one key habit — **consistency in the**

fundamentals. High performers don't need to think about fundamentals, as they have become their rituals.

Similarly, Jack Canfield, in his great book *The Success Principles,* says that **"99% is a bitch and 100% is a breeze."**

If you are required to use willpower to drag yourself out of bed to go to the gym every morning, then you will have a grueling time optimizing your performance. But if you become fully committed — and. with the use of initial willpower, build an exercise ritual — you'll hit the gym, just like brushing your teeth — without even thinking about it.

Here is the best advice. Instead of relying on willpower every time to get things done, use willpower initially to build habits and rituals, which will then take control of your days and weeks. As John Dryden rightly said, **"We first make our habits, and then habits make us."**

With rituals formed for most of their daily activities, high performers can do most of these activities without even thinking about them, which means they can do more in less time. They free up their mental space to be used for highly creative and chaotic activities, as the latter activities are undefined, and it's like getting into new territories — so such activities require most of our willpower and cognitive abilities.

By using willpower for the most important projects and finding solutions to the higher level of problems, you develop a greater sense of confidence, which empowers you to perform at a much better pace in your next level of pursuits.

Therefore, don't take your precious resource of willpower for granted. Instead, you should safeguard this priceless resource for your high-value activities by crafting rituals — and very soon, you will find yourself in the category of ultra-performers.

Chapter 6: Key Takeaways

It is essential to get crystal clear about your goals and why they are important to you, as they generate the necessary pull for you, but alongside, one needs to build necessary willpower to keep distractions at bay and build deep focus for longer periods to generate high-quality work. Here are a few scientifically-proven ways to boost your willpower:

Practice Daily Meditation

Neuroscience has proven that meditation is very helpful ***in staying focused, ignoring distractions, and controlling impulses.***

Mediation practice of ten to twenty minutes daily can set the tone for a productive day.

Exercise — the Wonder Drug for Willpower

Researchers have shown that a regular habit of doing exercise helps to reduce cravings. It not only relieves ordinary, everyday stress, but it's as ***powerful an antidepressant as Prozac.***

Any kind of regular exercise for half an hour can help you maintain great physical — as well as mental — health.

Use Self-Control Exercises

Treat your willpower like a muscle. Your physical muscles grow through exercise, you can also increase your willpower by practicing exercising your self-control on small and inconsequential things. This will boost your willpower in all areas of your life.

Precision and Specificity of Actions

Willpower depletes through vague directions. **The more specific you are about the timing and action to be taken, the more you will be able to use willpower to your advantage**.

Rituals to Safeguard Willpower

Instead of relying on willpower every time to get things done, use a bit of willpower initially to build habits and rituals, which then take control of your days and weeks. As John Dryden rightly said, ***"We first make our habits, and then habits make us."***

This spares a ton of willpower to strategically focus on our other most important pursuits.

Chapter 7: How to Activate High Performance in Everyday Life

****

"Without action, the best intentions in the world are nothing more than that: intentions."

– Jordan Belfort

A good life is nothing but a combination of intentionally well-lived days in a row for your entire life.

If we take care of our todays, we don't need to worry about our future, as when well-taken care of, today will bear the fruit in the form of better results in the future. Also, once we start taking care of days in a row – and then we look back – we will be able to see the wonderful past we have created. Therefore, a well-planned and well-lived day builds a strong foundation for a better tomorrow – and creates a fulfilling yesterday that you feel proud of.

To quote famous leadership expert, Robin Sharma: ***"Small daily improvements over time lead to stunning results."***

To continue to perform at our highest level, become intentional in planning your days. You need to keep your cravings for instant gratification at bay and focus on the activities that will help you move closer to your goals.

This section explains a few strategies that will help you take charge of your everyday actions. Let's look at these strategies now:

- **Apply the W.I.N. Formula to Control Your Moment-To-Moment Decisions**

What is the W.I.N. Formula?

This is the strategy that the highly successful use to take their moment-to-moment decisions, which enables them to craft their best days – and thus, achieve results.

W.I.N. stands for **what's important now**. This acronym was used by Bob Bowman, coach of legend Michael Phelps, an American swimmer and one of the most prized Olympic athletes in the History.

Phelps, in his book, *No Limits-The Will to Succeed,* explains the secrets behind all his legendary performances and winning of Olympic medals, including his coach's Bob Bowman strategies. He narrates an excerpt from his book where Coach Bowman explained **what**

separates Michael from all other swimmers.

Bowman stated that if other swimmers didn't feel good, they wouldn't swim – but this was not the case with Michael. He practiced and performed consistently, regardless of what he felt, as he has trained his mind through enough practice.

Phelps's behavior shows that high performers don't let their feelings get in the way of their actions. If something is to be done as a priority, then they perform at their best, regardless of what they feel in the moment about that activity. **Their feelings are not important; rather, the action towards the goal is important.**

It all depends on what is most important to you. As Ryan Blair once said, "If it is important to you, you'll find a way. If not, you'll find an excuse."

Most people give up under the influence of their impulses and instant gratification because they haven't spent enough time in getting clear about what is important to them. Once you get clear about what's important to you, you can move the mountain. As someone rightly said, clarity precedes success.

Phelps admits that his approach of giving preference to practice when others quit is based on the W.I.N. formula, which means that he thinks of '**what's important now**' instead of how he feels in the moment.

Therefore, it is this W.I.N. formula that motivates him to take positive action towards his goals, and with strong self-control and emotional mastery, he has been able to excel at this sport.

His conviction and commitment to what's important to him were evident when he said:

> *"It's true. When it comes down to it, when the time comes to focus and be mentally prepared, I can do whatever it takes to get there – in any situation."*

There is no ambiguity, no second thought in his mind – it's just a clear decision and strong commitment to follow life's priorities.

Guide Your Actions based on Your Future Self

Along similar lines of the W.I.N. Formula, Eric Greitens, a former Navy SEAL officer, writes in his book *Resilience: Hard-Won Wisdom for Living a Better Life,* that **your actions should be based on what you want to become, i.e.**

your future identity. It's never the right approach to act based on what you feel.

Simply put, your actions should be driven by the identity that you want to achieve and not by what you feel about the activity at any given point of time. The factor of feeling comes at the last in this formula. It goes like this:

Identity > Action > Feelings

Whenever you are in a dilemma about whether you should take some action or not, ask yourself, *"Who I want to become?"*

The answer to that question will guide you to take the right action – and that action will lead you closer to what you want to become. Now, with that sense of clarity about your direction, the level of energy you put in will be intense and massive – as compared to actions taken based on what you feel – and people can easily see the difference in the quality of actions you take when you are moving focused on building a future identity of yourself.

In the above equation, instead of making your feelings the dominant factor to take actions, you have simply put it at the end of the equation. Therefore, the whole sequence is reversed for your benefit, and now **your feelings become an outcome of actions taken by you**, guided by your future identity.

Therefore, the moral of the story is that you should not go by your feelings to decide your next action step – your emotions will simply leave you in a lurch.

If you are in a good mood one day, you might work your butt off; but the next day, if you don't feel better, you might just spoil your day. You'd agree that there are already so many uncontrollable outside factors to handle, and guiding your daily action based on what you feel will lead you nowhere. Taking action based on your feelings can never guarantee continuity, and, therefore, it's not a sustainable approach to deliver high performance.

Michael Phelps knew what he wanted to become – the best in the world in his game. **Thus, the W.I.N. principle guided him to take the right action for him to attain that identity of a world-class swimmer**.

The actions taken on the right underlying factors lead to a performance at a heightened level, which delivers the best results. So finally, with your goal achieved, and you FEEL superb now – and that's the way to go.

What kind of action leads to high performance?

Okay, let's take it one step further.

So far, based on the identity you have chosen for yourself, apply the W.I.N. formula to take the immediate action that's most important for you. Since we are talking about achieving the state of high performance; it is quite relevant here to talk about the level and quality of actions to be taken more specifically.

Grant Cardone, in his book, *The 10X Rule*, addresses this point:

"One question I've received over the years is, 'Exactly how much action is necessary to create success?' Not surprisingly, everyone is looking for the secret shortcut—and equally unsurprising is the following fact: There are no shortcuts. **The more action you take, the better your chances are of getting a break**. *Disciplined, consistent, and persistent actions are more of a determining factor in the creation of success than any other combination of things.* **Understanding how to calculate and then take the right amount of action is more important than your concept, idea, invention, or business plan**"

Grant further states that most people fail because they are operating at the wrong degree of action. He goes on to **categorize the actions based on their degree of involvement;** anyone can make any of **these four choices to take action**:

    1. Do nothing.

    2. Retreat.

    3. Take normal levels of action.

4. Take massive action.

Cardone recommends choosing massive action when he says: *'Overcommit, be all in, and take massive levels of action followed up by massive amounts of more actions.* ***You will create new problems and deliver at levels that will amaze even you.****"*

Be clear in your mind that any lukewarm actions will give you provide mediocre results. If you keep on doing routine activities and take normal levels of action, you can't create the required momentum needed for performing at higher levels.

In fact, you might end up deceiving yourself here; it will falsely convince you that you are already taking action – but such actions never bring high-quality results, so you end up remaining a below-average performer.

There, the high-performance mantra is shaping your future identity – what you want to become, and then disregarding your feelings and taking massive actions by applying the W.I.N. formula.

Now let's talk about the next strategy to incorporate high performance into your daily life.

Set Product Goals and Process Goals.

We all have heard enough about goal setting. There is enough literature out there teaching you that you should SMART goals, with the essential features of being:

- Specific
- Measurable
- Attainable
- Relevant
- Time-bound

But the key problem with such goals is that they are only outcome-based and to be attained in the future only. For most people, this becomes the very reason that they fail to achieve their goals; they think they still have time to achieve their goals in the future, but they don't know how to decide those actions that will lead to achieving those goals. That's why you see that most people set almost the same goals every year – as they fail to hit those goals year after year.

The solution lies in setting two categories of goals, as Jason Selk, a leading peak performance coach suggests. They are:

1. Product goals
2. Process goals

Product goals are <u>result oriented</u> and potentially attainable within twelve months. For example, if you have a goal of running a half-marathon in the next six months or a full marathon in twelve months, that will be your product goal. **Product goals are specific in terms of results and the timelines to attain those goals**.

Process goals are <u>action-oriented</u> – they focus on **what actions need to be taken daily to achieve your product goals.** It is vital to set the process goal for every product goal because it is very easy to set up a goal that is far away six months or one year, but when we see the goal still a few months away, we tend to drift.

We think that we will be able to catch up sooner on those goals when we reach closer to the deadline. But it doesn't work that way – because if we start drifting, that becomes a vicious circle. Skipping one day leads to skipping another day, and soon, you realize that you have not worked for days, weeks, or even months and that you've been giving excuses for your inactivity. Here, process goals come to your rescue.

"<u>Set</u> Product Goals and <u>Emphasize</u> Process Goals: To achieve greatness, you must set end goals and place

significant emphasis on what it takes to accomplish them."

~ Jason Selk

Jason recommends that **we should have two or three process goals for each of the product goals**. Sometimes a process goal may happen less frequently than every day, but it still needs to occur regularly to drive the achievement of the product goal. Take your previous example of running a half marathon six months from now; as your product goal, what should be your process goal?

Here, you need to have two to three process goals, and those could be as per below:

a. Rigorously follow a **daily running and exercise schedule**, including the provisions for recovery days.
b. **Consume a healthy diet/nutrients** daily and avoid junk food.
c. **Regularly go through a training guide** or consult a fitness coach – if you have engaged one – to ensure that you are following the training correctly to avoid any injuries.

Process goals are the immediate motivators that spur you into daily action that will bring you closer to achieving the distant product goal. Setting up both product and process goals will not only give you a sense of direction but also ensure that you are on the right track and achieving regular progress.

While product goals bring you to the flag at the summit of the mountain, process goals motivate you and establish a plan that will inspire you to keep climbing every day.

Process goals also help to prevent you from becoming demotivated due to the distant nature of your goals; this daily progress will ultimately lead to your product goals.

Chapter 7: Key Takeaways

The achievement of your important goals takes time, and it requires mastering your daily actions and ensuring that you continue to take action without procrastination or becoming carried away by your feelings or emotions. High performers follow certain principles, such as those stated below, to consistently take daily actions towards achieving their goals.

Apply the W.I.N. Formula to Control Your Moment to Moment Decisions:

W.I.N. stands for **"What's Important Now."**

Michael Phelps, an American swimmer and the most-prized Olympics Gold Medalist, follows this formula. Instead of being guided by his feelings, Phelps chooses to take action based on what's important in a particular moment that will bring him closer to achieving his goals.

Guide Your Actions Based on the Future Identity You Want to Create

Decide what you want to create for yourself in the future. The more committed you are to your future identity, the more your actions will be guided by your future self. And then your feelings will be the outcome of those actions. Once you know that your actions are directing you towards your goals and will help to make you the kind of person you want to become, you'll generate feelings of fulfilment.

Therefore, don't let your feelings guide your actions. Decide what type of identity you want to create for yourself, ask yourself what's important from moment to moment, and let that process guide your actions.

- **Set Product Goals and Process Goals Simultaneously**

Most people set goals based on the outcome they want to achieve – this outcome could be related to their finances, health, or career, for example – but they lack the necessary action plan and commitment to achieve those goals. That's why setting both product goals and process goals becomes important

Product goals are **result-oriented** and **potentially attainable over the next 12 months**.

Process goals are **action-oriented** goals – they focus on **what actions need to be taken on a daily or more regular basis** to achieve your product goals.

Chapter 8: The Neuroscience of the "Flow" State and How to Experience it More Often

****

"The happiest people spend much time in a state of flow — the state in which people are so involved in an activity that nothing else seems to matter; the experience itself is so enjoyable that people will do it even at great cost, for the sheer sake of doing it."

~ Mihaly Csikszentmihalyi

Perhaps you (or others you know) have experienced a state of consciousness when you seemed to be working effortlessly, and time seemed to flow quickly; it often happens when you are engaged in something that you really care about and enjoy doing — it's called a state of flow when you work at higher levels of consciousness. Different names are given to this state of consciousness, such as "runner's high", "being in the zone", or "peak performance".

"Flow" is defined by researchers as an **optimal state of consciousness, those highest moments of total absorption in our activity — in such a way that we lose our own sense of existence**. In such states of consciousness, time seems to fly, and an individual's performance goes through the roof. The world's greatest thinkers have described **the state of flow as the most productive and creative state of mind — one in which work doesn't remain work anymore; rather, it becomes a joy**.

I think of this as a state when there is no difference between the doer and doing — they become inseparable. For example, when a dancer gets into the state of flow, she forgets any difference between herself and dance. The dancer becomes the dance. It is a situation of complete immersion in the activity, where your entire focus is on the activity, and you become insulated from any kind of distractions.

The above experiences might seem mystical or esoteric to a few people. Also, the topic of flow may not sound like a sober scientific topic to most people to be researched deeply. Fortunately, there have been a few wonderful people who were curious to research this deeply and to understand the science behind it and how it feels when someone experiences that state of being.

Hungarian psychologist Mihaly Csikszentmihalyi pioneered the research on this psychological concept of a highly-focused mental state that is conducive to the highest levels of individual performance. He recognized and coined this heightened state of consciousness as "flow". Here is what he did.

Csikszentmihalyi studied many people to understand the state of flow and how it felt when someone experienced such a state. In one of his talks[14], he described that based on his studies and **interviews of more than *eight thousand* people** around the world — from Dominican monks to blind nuns, to Himalayan climbers, to Navajo shepherds — who enjoy their work, regardless of their culture, education, etc., he found that below are the **characteristics of any person when he or she is in a state of flow**:

- **Completely immersed** in what they are doing – focused and concentrated.
- A deep **sense of ecstasy** — of being outside everyday reality.

14

https://www.ted.com/talks/mihaly_csikszentmihalyi_on_flow

- Greater **inner clarity** — knowing what needs to be done, and how well they are doing it.
- **Knowing that the activity is doable** — that their skills are adequate for the task.
- A **sense of serenity** — no worries about oneself and a feeling of growing beyond the boundaries of the age.
- **Timelessness** — thoroughly focused on the present, hours seem to pass by in minutes.
- Intrinsically motivated — **whatever activity produces flow becomes its own reward**.

Just try to imagine such a state — a state of ultimate joy and pleasure. The best part is that the levels of performance are undoubtedly of the highest quality and at an excitingly fast pace.

Neuroscience Shows What Happens in a Brain in the Flow State

As of now, scientists have made enormous progress in their research about the flow state. Advancements in brain-imaging technologies have allowed them to apply serious metrics on this internal state of being, which was earlier a subjective experience. Neuroscience has established that it can measure the state of flow in our brains by using electromyographic signals (EMF) technology.

The science behind peak human performance[15] shows that the state of flow emerges from a radical al**teration in normal brain function. In the flow, as attention heightens, the slower and energy-expensive extrinsic system (conscious processing) is swapped out for the far faster and more efficient processing of the subconscious, intrinsic system.**

Arne Dietrich, a neuroscientist at the American University of Beirut who helped discover this phenomenon of transition, described this as an ***efficiency exchange***. He states, "We're trading energy usually used for higher cognitive functions for heightened attention and awareness."

The technical term for this efficiency exchange is "***transient hypofrontality***," with "hypo" (meaning slow) (being the opposite of "hyper" (i.e., fast)) and "frontal" referring to the prefrontal cortex, the part of our brain that houses our higher cognitive functions. This is one of the main reasons flow feels flowy — because any brain structure that would hamper rapid-fire decision-making is shut off.

---

[15] http://time.com/56809/the-science-of-peak-human-performance/

More precisely, three specific internal changes have been noted by neuroscientists in this:

1. **The de-activation of the dorsolateral prefrontal cortex:** In 2008, for example, Dr. Charles Limb, a surgeon and neuroscientist, used functional magnetic resonance imaging (fMRI) to examine the brains of improv jazz musicians in the flow. He found the **dorsolateral prefrontal cortex (DLPFC), an area of the brain best known for self-monitoring, deactivated**. Self-monitoring is the voice of doubt, also known as our inner critic — the worst enemy when you try to achieve anything big. Since flow is a fluid state — where problem-solving is nearly automatic — second-guessing can only slow down that process. When the DLPFC goes silent, the source of self-doubt or second-guessing shuts off — the result is the state of liberation. We act without hesitation. **Creativity becomes more free-flowing, risk-taking becomes less fearful, and the combination lets us flow at a far faster pace**. It is pertinent to note here that cardio exercise re-directs blood flow far away from the DLPFC to the motor parts of the brain, enabling a more embodied focus without interference from self-consciousness, distraction, or negative thinking.

2. **Change in the brainwaves:** Not only does the DLPFC become quiet, but in the state of flow, the function of our brainwaves changes. In

the state of flow, we shift from the fast-moving beta waves (frequency of 12 to 38 Hz) of waking consciousness down to the **far slower borderline between alpha and theta (8Hz and below)**.

Alpha is daydreaming mode — when we slip from idea to idea without much internal resistance. Theta, meanwhile, only shows up during rapid eye movement (REM) sleep or just before we fall asleep, in that hypnogogic gap where ideas combine in truly radical ways. Theta is our gateway to learning, memory, and intuition. **In theta, our senses are withdrawn from the external world and focused on signals originating from within**. These slower brainwaves help us to get the maximum benefits of our cognitive abilities and speed up our decision-making process.

3. **Release of pleasure-inducing neurochemicals:** Besides the two above changes, i.e. the quieting of the DLFPC and change in the brainwaves, finally, there's neurochemistry of flow. A team of neuroscientists at Bonn University in Germany discovered that **endorphins are released** during the state of flow. Also, other researchers have determined that additionally, the brain releases other chemicals, such as **norepinephrine, dopamine, anandamide, and serotonin in the state of flow**.

All these five components are pleasure-inducing, performance-enhancing neurochemicals, upping everything from **muscle reaction times to attention, pattern recognition and lateral thinking** — the crucial elements for rapid-fire problem-solving.

Taken together, all these above changes in brain function provided the scientists with an exceptionally potent workaround for the problem of teaching people how to be more creative. Instead of finding some outside stimulants or circumstances to address this question, we can instead improve people's ability to find flow, and the state's neurobiology takes care of the rest. Researchers have already credited flow with most athletic gold medals and world championships, major scientific breakthroughs, and significant progress in the arts.

In a 10-year McKinsey study[16], top executives reported being five times more productive in the state of flow. You can focus better because the inner critic becomes silent, and then nothing can distract you in that state of flow.

---

[16] https://www.mckinsey.com/business-functions/organization/our-insights/increasing-the-meaning-quotient-of-work

How to Experience More of the State of Flow

Isn't it astonishing that by harnessing the brain's innate capacity, the interplay of neurochemistry, and the transition of brainwaves, our mental capacity becomes so flowy that one can perform at heightened levels for longer hours?

Is there any way to enjoy the state of flow — which increases over time — more often, so you can consistently perform at higher levels and deliver exceptional returns?

Yes, it's possible.

Csikszentmihalyi, in his great book, *Flow*, gives a tested principle to achieve the flow state more often. He explains that the game of flow is all about making the right kind of balance between the level of your skill set and the challenges you want to handle. He states:

*"In all the activities people in our study reported engaging in, **enjoyment comes at a very specific point: whenever the opportunities for action perceived by the individual are equal to his or her capabilities**. Playing tennis, for instance, is not enjoyable if the two opponents are mismatched. The less skilled player will feel anxious, and the better player will feel bored. The same is true for every other activity. **Enjoyment appears at the boundary***

between boredom and anxiety *when the challenges are just balanced with the person's capacity to act."*

Csikszentmihalyi further states that:

*"The optimal state of inner experience is one in which there is an order in consciousness. This happens when **psychic energy—or attention—is invested in realistic goals, and when skills match the opportunities for action**. The pursuit of a goal brings order in awareness because a person must concentrate attention on the task at hand and momentarily forget everything else. **These periods of struggling to overcome challenges are what people find to be the most enjoyable of their lives**. A person who has achieved control over their psychic energy and has invested it in consciously chosen goals cannot help but grow into a more complex being. By stretching skills, by reaching toward higher challenges, such a person becomes an increasingly extraordinary individual."*

Also, Leo Babauta, a blogger at zenhabits.net, beautifully states certain steps[17] that can help you to achieve this wonderful state of flow:

---

[17] https://zenhabits.net/guide-to-achieving-flow-and-happiness-in-your-work/

- **Choose work you love**. If you dread a task, you'll have a hard time losing yourself in it. If your job is made up of stuff you hate, you might want to consider finding another job. Or consider seeking projects you love to do within your current job. At any rate, be sure that whatever task you choose is something you can be passionate about.

- **Choose an important task**. There's work you love that's easy and unimportant, and then there's work you love that will make a long-term impact on your career and life. Choose the latter, as it will be a much better use of your time, and you can get into a state of flow.

- **Make sure it's challenging, but not too hard**. If a task is too easy, you will be able to complete it without much thought or effort. A task should be challenging enough to require your full concentration. However, if it is too hard, you will find it difficult to lose yourself in it, as you will spend most of your concentration just trying to figure out how to do it. It may take some trial and error to find tasks of the appropriate level of difficulty.

- **Find your quiet, peak time**. First, you'll want to find a quiet time, or you'll never be able to focus. That might be early morning when you have just woken up, or early in the workday, when most people haven't arrived yet or are still getting their coffee and settling down. Or you might try the lunch hour, when people are usually out of the office. Evenings work well, too, for many people. Or, if you're lucky, you can do it at any time of the day if you can find a quiet spot to work in. Whatever time you choose, it should also be a peak energy time for you. Find a time when you have lots of energy and can concentrate.

- **Clear away distractions**. Aside from finding a quiet time and place to work, you'll want to clear away all other distractions. That means turning off distracting music (unless you find music that helps you focus), turning off phones, email, and Facebook, Twitter notifications, and anything else that might pop up or make noise to interrupt your thoughts.

- **Learn to focus on that task for as long as possible**. This takes practice. You need to start on your chosen task and keep your focus on it for as long as you can. At first, many people will have difficulty, if they're used to constantly switching between tasks. But keep trying and keep bringing your focus back to your task. You'll get better. And if you can keep your focus on that task, with no distractions, and if your task has been chosen well (something you love, something important, and something challenging), you would find yourself lost yourself in flow soon.

- **Keep practicing**. Again, this takes practice. Each step will take some practice, from finding a quiet, peak time for yourself, to clearing distractions, to choosing the right task — and especially keeping your focus on a task for a long time. But each time you fail, try to learn from it. Each time you succeed, you should also learn from it — what did you do right? And the more you practice, the better you'll get.

- **Reap the rewards**. Aside from the pleasure of getting into a flow state, you'll also be happier with your work overall. You'll get important stuff done. You'll complete stuff more often, rather than starting and stopping frequently. All of this is hugely satisfying and rewarding. Take the time to appreciate this and to continue to practice it every day.

All the strategies mentioned in the book will help you build a better self-image and improve your focus by not giving in to distractions and temptations. They also definitely play a significant role in putting you on the fast track to achieve high performance.

I've intentionally stated the concept of flow at the end of this book because once you have mastered what we have covered in all the previous sections, you'll be already equipped with key tools like enhanced focus to work for longer hours and boosted willpower to keep distraction at bay, and, therefore, you will attract more flow while engaging in your most important goals.

Chapter 8: Key Takeaways

The peak for a high performer is to experience flow while doing their most important things.

'Flow' is an **optimal state of consciousness — those highest moments of total absorption in the activity we are into — in such a way that we lose our own sense of existence**.

The characteristics of any person when he/she is in a state of flow are:

- Complete **immersion** in what they are doing
- A deep sense of **ecstasy**
- Greater **inner clarity**
- Knowing that the activity is **doable**
- A sense of **serenity**
- **Timelessness**
- **Intrinsic** motivation

Neuroscience of What Happens in the Brain in Flow State:

Three specific internal changes have been noted by neuroscientists when someone is in the state of flow:

- **De-activation of Dorsolateral Prefrontal Cortex** an area of the brain best known for self-monitoring, deactivated. Creativity becomes more free-flowing, risk-taking becomes less fearful, and that combination lets us flow at a far faster pace.

- Change in the brainwaves to the **more relaxed brainwaves of alpha and theta, wherein you can** listen deeply to the inner wisdom that enhances your cognitive abilities and speeds up the decision-making process.

- **Release of pleasure-inducing neurochemicals** like endorphins, norepinephrine, dopamine, anandamide, and serotonin.

How to Experience Flow State More Often

You can experience the state of flow in any task where there an optimal match between the level of the challenge and your level of skills. If the task is too challenging vis-à-vis the level of your skills, you become anxious — and if there is a low challenge compared to your skills, it becomes boring. Flow arrives **when the challenges are just balanced with the person's capacity to act**.

Steps to Get into the State of Flow

- Choose work you love.
- Choose an important task.
- Make sure it's challenging, but not too hard.
- Find your quiet, peak time.
- Clear away distractions.
- Learn to focus on that task for as long as possible.
- Keep practicing.

Closing Thoughts

****

"Successful people do what unsuccessful people are not willing to do."

~ Jeff Olson

I sincerely hope you have learned enough principles and practical strategies to attain expertise in any skill and perform at your best levels.

You know there are no outside factors that prevent you from reaching your best potential. In fact, psychology and neuroscience have already shown you the vast potential of the human body and mind. You have everything within you to enhance your level of performance and achieve any heights you choose for yourself through deliberate practice.

Therefore, I urge you not to let whatever knowledge you have gained to just wither away. Only you can turn this knowledge into your personal wisdom.

Someone once said, "Knowledge is power". But this is not entirely true. Knowledge is only potential power. The **real power emerges**

when you apply the acquired knowledge to form definite plans of action and take action towards your important goals.

You don't need to do it all at once. Just pick one strategy or practice today and start imbibing it into your daily life. The principles you have been exposed to in this book have already implemented by high achievers; they work, so they will work for you too. You just need to set the right intention and start taking action.

I wish you a life of mastery and excellence in all your pursuits.

Cheers

May I ask you for a small favor?

At the outset, I want to give you a big thanks for taking out time to read this book. You could have chosen any other book, but you took mine, and I totally appreciate this.

I hope you got at least a few actionable insights that will have a positive impact on your day to day life.

Can I ask for 30 seconds more of your time?

I'd love if you could leave a review about the book at Amazon. Reviews may not matter to big-name authors; but they're a tremendous help for authors like me, who don't have much following. They help me to grow my readership by encouraging folks to take a chance on my books.

To put it straight– **reviews are the life blood for any author.**

It will just take less than a minute of your time, but will tremendously help me to reach out to more people, so please leave your review.

Thanks for your support to my work. And I'd love to see your review.

Full Book Summary

CHAPTER 1: KEY TAKEAWAYS

High performance, as astutely defined by Brendon Burchard, is consistently performing and delivering results above and beyond standard norms over the long-term.

High performers are not necessarily the ones who become so because of genetics or their natural talent. Human biology is governed by certain principles that enable anyone to excel in their performance.

Barring a few genetic constraints, for the most part, the human body and mind can be very well stated **as a normalizing machine**. If, over time, you expose humans to a different set of environments or circumstances, they can adapt and perform in any circumstances. Two principles that govern this human adaptability are:

- **Homeostasis:**

Homeostasis is a characteristic of a system that regulates its internal environment and tends to maintain a stable, relatively constant condition of properties.

When we push ourselves beyond what is comfortable for our bodies, our bodies respond by overcompensating in the pursuit of creating a new higher level of homeostasis.

- **Neuroplasticity**

Neuroplasticity refers to the **ability of the human brain to reorganize itself, both physically and functionally, due to your environment, behavior, thinking, and emotions** — irrespective of age, gender, demography, location, etc.

The principles of homeostasis and neuroplasticity give enough confidence that our bodies and brains are capable of performing well beyond our self-created false limits. By merely becoming aware of these principles, helps anyone to start thinking differently about themselves and their capacities.

CHAPTER 2: KEY TAKEAWAYS

Despite being aware of the principle of the malleability of our human bodies and brains, most people fail to make the changes necessary to lead a better life.

The key reason why people fail to transform is their self-image. They can't act beyond what they perceive as their own self-image, and they run their lives based on the identities they have created for themselves.

Your identity precedes your activity.

Your self-image can be divided into two parts (1) Social roles; and (2) Personality Traits, as identified by social psychologist, Manfred Kuhn.

If your self-image is not serving, and you fail to take charge of your life, it's time to change your life.

Lanny Bassham, Olympic Gold Medalist in shooting and a high-performance enthusiast based on his talks with hundreds of sports personalities, concluded that **all the high performers attribute 90% of their success to the mental game**. He proposes a two-part formula to change your self-image, as per below:

- **Mental Rehearsal**

In this approach, you mentally rehearse performing that task in the most effective way, see yourself making the perfect move, and see yourself succeeding always.

- **A personal statement:** *"I do it all the time."* + *"That's like me."*

These affirmation statements imprint your new identity of high performance in your brain.

Surround yourself with people who evoke a sense of faith in you, and minimize the time you spend with negative people.

CHAPTER 3: KEY TAKEAWAYS

Taking action at the highest level is largely a mental game; it requires you to make certain mental shifts, so that you start to think differently and, therefore, perceive situations differently before taking any actions. The key mental shifts are:

- **Take stress as a challenge, not as a threat.**

There are two kinds of stress. One that most people consider in the negative sense is distress, which is non-resourceful; however, there is a resourceful kind of stress known as "Eustress" — good stress that prepares you to accept the situation and rise to the challenge to achieve your goals.

Merely perceiving stress differently affects your neurochemistry. If you consider any kind of stress to be a threat, it releases a hormone called 'cortisol', which puts you into a fearful mode. But merely by perceiving stress as a challenge, you get a dose of DHEA, a neurosteroid that puts you into action mode to face the situation positively.

Dale Carnegie's offers his **formula to beat 90% of the stress in just four simple steps** as per below:

> 5. *Writing down precisely what I am worried about.*
> 6. *Writing down what I can do about it.*
> 7. *Deciding what to do.*
> 8. *Starting immediately to carry out that decision.*

- **Use consistent thought replacement from moment to moment.**

The idea behind consistent thought replacement is **to observe your thoughts from moment to moment and direct them towards your desired goal**; don't let your mind wander with some negative thoughts or criticism or mere distractions.

- **Master the moments between stimulus and response.**

Viktor Frankl, stated, *"Between stimulus and response there is a space. In that space is our power to choose our response. In our response lies our growth and our freedom."*

Instead of acting on our impulses and reacting immediately, we must realize that there is always some space between the stimulus that triggered our emotions and the way that we respond to that. If we master the tiny spaces between stimulus and response and choose the right actions, it will significantly enhance the quality of our lives.

- **Safeguard yourself from mind pollution from technological gadgets.**

Most of us, in our waking hours, are almost always surrounded by people, various forms of technology, and gadgets. Somehow, we still can manage to get away from other people after finishing our work-related duties, but technology and modern-day gadgets like smartphones and television are difficult to escape from.

For the most part, technological gadgets are made by for-profit companies to make people addicted to the screens so that they can sell their own products/servies or others' advertisements, as indicated by experts who have worked for such companies.

Performing at higher levels requires focus and undivided attention on the difficult goals for a longer time, so you can get into a state of flow, and, therefore, any distractions that can disturb your mind with non-resourceful information or cheap entertainment must be avoided.

Therefore, be smart with your smartphone, and turn off the television.

CHAPTER 4: KEY TAKEAWAYS

You can't perform at excellent levels – and, therefore, can't grow faster – if you don't focus on acquiring new skills or upgrade your existing skills to the next level.

But you don't want to spend ages learning or upgrading your skills, and you need some effective techniques to develop skills faster. Here are some key ways you can acquire any skills faster and sustainably:

- **The principle of stress and recovery for growth**

The formula for growth in any area of life is to expose yourself to stress but also ensure that you recover well. Here is the growth equation looks like:

Stress + Recovery = Growth

As rightly stated by performance psychologist Jim Loehr, "...*Stress is the stimulus for growth. Recovery is when you grow.*"

But don't overstretch yourself while stressing out – rather, take on manageable challenges. Use the Goldilocks principle, which means that something is 'just right'. We should be stretching but not snapping. We are at the threshold where growth occurs without injury.

Steve Kotler suggests the magic stretch number as four percent beyond your existing capacity. He says: "***If we want to achieve the kinds of accelerated performance we're seeing in action and adventure sports, then it's 4 percent plus 4 percent plus 4 percent, day after day, week after week, months into years into careers…***"

Also, try to introduce rest, even into high-stake environments or complex situations, by slowing down your breathing and relaxing; you'll be able to make better decisions.

- **Travel between the learning and performance zones.**

Learning doesn't end when you finish school or college, it's a life-long journey.

Even after you have started your career, don't just rely on merely getting experience in your performance zone. Instead, **you should often travel between the performance and learning zones to improve the quality of**

your work by implementing the new ways as you continuously learn.

CHAPTER 5: KEY TAKEAWAYS

Mere practice doesn't make your perfect; rather, you must practice with the right set of knowledge and tools to attain expertise and become a master in your chosen domain.

Anders Ericsson, a researcher and psychologist at Florida State University, explained there are **three types of practices** people pursue to gain any skill in any field, as stated below:

- **Naive practice**

Naive practice is a **generic kind of mindless practice**, where you simply keep on doing what you have already learned.

This is the case where *twenty* years of experience in a particular field is nothing but one year of experience just repeated over *twenty* years without learning anything new.

- **Purposeful practice** has the following features.

    a. **Well-defined and specific goals**.
    b. Purposeful practice is **<u>focused</u>**.

c. Purposeful practice **requires feedback.**
   d. Purposeful practice **gets out of your comfort zone.**

- **Deliberate practice.**

This practice has all the elements of the purposeful practice – but, **additionally, it has the element of coaching or teaching added to it through a clear training program** in the established field.

Deliberate practice changes internal brain structure

Deliberate practice for a number of years **changes the neural circuitry of the practitioner's brains to produce highly specialized mental representations**, which, in turn, make possible the incredible **memory, pattern recognition, problem-solving, and other advanced abilities** needed to excel in their particular specialties.

CHAPTER 6: KEY TAKEAWAYS

It is essential to get crystal clear about your goals and why they are important to you, as they generate the necessary pull for you, but alongside, one needs to build necessary willpower to keep distractions at bay and build deep focus for longer periods to generate high-quality work. Here are a few scientifically-proven ways to boost your willpower:

Practice Daily Meditation

Neuroscience has proven that meditation is very helpful *in staying focused, ignoring distractions, and controlling impulses.*

Mediation practice of ten to twenty minutes daily can set the tone for a productive day.

Exercise — the Wonder Drug for Willpower

Researchers have shown that a regular habit of doing exercise helps to reduce cravings. It not only relieves ordinary, everyday stress, but it's as *powerful an antidepressant as Prozac.*

Any kind of regular exercise for half an hour can help you maintain great physical — as well as mental — health.

Use Self-Control Exercises

Treat your willpower like a muscle. Your physical muscles grow through exercise, you can also increase your willpower by practicing exercising your self-control on small and inconsequential things. This will boost your willpower in all areas of your life.

Precision and Specificity of Actions

Willpower depletes through vague directions. **The more specific you are about the timing and action to be taken, the more you will be able to use willpower to your advantage**.

Rituals to Safeguard Willpower

Instead of relying on willpower every time to get things done, use a bit of willpower initially to build habits and rituals, which then take control of your days and weeks. As John Dryden rightly said, ***"We first make our habits, and then habits make us."***

This spares a ton of willpower to strategically focus on our other most important pursuits.

CHAPTER 7: KEY TAKEAWAYS

The achievement of your important goals takes time, and it requires mastering your daily actions and ensuring that you continue to take action without procrastination or becoming carried away by your feelings or emotions. High performers follow certain principles, such as those stated below, to consistently take daily actions towards achieving their goals.

Apply the W.I.N. Formula to Control Your Moment to Moment Decisions:

W.I.N. stands for **"What's Important Now."**

Michael Phelps, an American swimmer and the most-prized Olympics Gold Medalist, follows this formula. Instead of being guided by his feelings, Phelps chooses to take action based on what's important in a particular moment that will bring him closer to achieving his goals.

Guide Your Actions Based on the Future Identity You Want to Create

Decide what you want to create for yourself in the future. The more committed you are to your future identity, the more your actions will be guided by your future self. And then your feelings will be the outcome of those actions. Once you know that your actions are directing you towards your goals and will help to make you the kind of person you want to become, you'll generate feelings of fulfilment.

Therefore, don't let your feelings guide your actions. Decide what type of identity you want to create for yourself, ask yourself what's important from moment to moment, and let that process guide your actions.

- **Set Product Goals and Process Goals Simultaneously**

Most people set goals based on the outcome they want to achieve – this outcome could be related to their finances, health, or career, for example –

but they lack the necessary action plan and commitment to achieve those goals. That's why setting both product goals and process goals becomes important

Product goals are **result-oriented** and **potentially attainable over the next 12 months**.

Process goals are **action-oriented** goals – they focus on **what actions need to be taken on a daily or more regular basis** to achieve your product goals.

CHAPTER 8: KEY TAKEAWAYS

The peak for a high performer is to experience flow while doing their most important things.

'Flow' is an **optimal state of consciousness — those highest moments of total absorption in the activity we are into — in such a way that we lose our own sense of existence**.

The characteristics of any person when he/she is in a state of flow are:

- Complete **immersion** in what they are doing
- A deep sense of **ecstasy**
- Greater **inner clarity**
- Knowing that the activity is **doable**

- A sense of **serenity**
- **Timelessness**
- **Intrinsic** motivation

Neuroscience of What Happens in the Brain in Flow State:

Three specific internal changes have been noted by neuroscientists when someone is in the state of flow:

- **De-activation of Dorsolateral Prefrontal Cortex** an area of the brain best known for self-monitoring, deactivated. Creativity becomes more free-flowing, risk-taking becomes less fearful, and that combination lets us flow at a far faster pace.

- Change in the brainwaves to the **more relaxed brainwaves of alpha and theta, wherein you can** listen deeply to the inner wisdom that enhances your cognitive abilities and speeds up the decision-making process.

- **Release of pleasure-inducing neurochemicals** like endorphins, norepinephrine, dopamine, anandamide, and serotonin.

How to Experience Flow State More Often

You can experience the state of flow in any task where there an optimal match between the level of the challenge and your level of skills. If the task is too challenging vis-à-vis the level of your skills, you become anxious — and if there is a low challenge compared to your skills, it becomes boring. Flow arrives **when the challenges are just balanced with the person's capacity to act**.

Steps to Get into the State of Flow

- Choose work you love.
- Choose an important task.
- Make sure it's challenging, but not too hard.
- Find your quiet, peak time.
- Clear away distractions.
- Learn to focus on that task for as long as possible.
- Keep practicing.

Could you please leave a review on the book?

One last time!

I'd love if you could leave a review about the book at Amazon. Reviews may not matter to big-name authors; but they're a tremendous help for authors like me, who don't have much following. They help me to grow my readership by encouraging folks to take a chance on my books.

To put it straight– **reviews are the life blood for any author.**

It will just take less than a minute of yours, but will tremendously help me to reach out to more people, so please leave your review.

Thank you for supporting my work and I'd love to see your review on the book.

Preview of the book "Intelligent Thinking"

Introduction

****

"The world we have created is a product of our thinking; it cannot be changed without changing our thinking."

~ Albert Einstein

It was year 2002. He had just sold his stakes in a high-tech online payment company that brought him a hefty multi-million dollar fortune in his early thirties. Despite attaining a huge success at such a young age, he didn't do it all just to enjoy sunning at beaches and doing nothing for the rest of his life.

This is Elon Musk, who had further crazy plans for his life and mankind. As a serial entrepreneur, his next move was to build something tangible in the real world that could change the world. Despite his past experience in internet business, now he was thinking beyond the earth and getting into the space business, with the objective of seeing the possibility of human life on other planets and even a human colony on Mars.

The next step was to find out how to travel in space – obviously through rocket technology. But the cheapest US rocket would have cost him no less than 65 million US dollars, and he needed a few of these to initiate research to see the possibility of life on Mars. In his search for affordable technology, he traveled to Russia and initiated discussions with a few rocket companies to explore buying rockets from them. But the cheapest rockets would still cost no less than 15-20 million US dollars each and that was even without any nukes. The crux of the matter was that even the hardest negotiations wouldn't have yielded him close to what he was looking for. He realized that he might end up spending everything he had made from the sale of his stakes in Paypal, without a clear sign of recovering it, if he went ahead with buying rockets from outside.

Had he been someone else, he might have become frustrated and just quit at such roadblocks, but not Musk. So what did he do? He thought differently. He started exploring whether he could make rockets by himself despite his lack of experience in a new domain that was entirely different from what he had done during entire life so far. The next step was to dig him deeper into learning what this space technology was all about and how it operated. It was definitely a mammoth task for any internet entrepreneur to even fathom the thought of cracking space technology, but Musk, after many failures and almost losing his entire life earnings, finally cracked the code, and today his company SpaceX is a preferred vendor for huge orders of space rockets from the United States government.

Can you imagine Musk's internal thinking process, when he was contemplating manufacturing rockets? In one interview, he explained how he thought about and looked at the problem of manufacturing rockets on his own[18]:

"I tend to approach things from a physics framework. And physics teaches you to **reason from first principles rather**

---

[18] https://www.wired.com/2012/10/ff-elon-musk-qa/

than by analogy. So I said, OK, let's look at the first principles. What is a rocket made of? Aerospace-grade aluminum alloys, plus some titanium, copper, and carbon fiber. And then I asked, what is the value of those materials on the commodity market? It turned out that the materials cost of a rocket was around 2 percent of the typical price—which is a crazy ratio for a large mechanical product."

Musk's first principle thinking was along the lines of the laws of physics – this means you need to first deconstruct the final product into its core ingredients and then see how differently you can work with these core constituents and produce something out of it. This kind of first principle thinking was used by history's great thinkers, including the ancient philosopher, Aristotle; but probably no one embodies the philosophy of first principle thinking at such a vast level more than Elon Musk.

Unfortunately, most people just see success as a series of "events", and they don't pay the required attention to the "process" that leads to the success– it involves sincere thinking at a granular level before you achieve the clarity of approach to reach your goals.

Investment legend, Warren Buffett, also gives credit for his entire success to developing the thinking abilities that enabled him to make the right investment decisions most of the time. He says, "I insist on a lot of time being spent, almost every day, to just sit and think. That is very uncommon in American business. I read and think. So I **do more reading and thinking**, and make less impulse decisions than most people in business. I do it because I like this kind of life."

The important question that arises here is what makes these high-achievers different from other people that puts them into an entirely different league – in a way that people start to see these people as super human? In fact, it is simply that they learn how to use an important human endowment- the human ability to think clearly and intelligently.

They know the pitfalls or flaws of older conditioned ways of thinking. They choose to disassociate themselves from the limitations of this thinking and make a conscious choice to read and learn the newer way, and thus they create different and unique outcomes for themselves.

They are strong believers in the natural principle, as stated by Stephen R. Covey, that everything is built twice – first in the mind and then in the real world. If you can learn to think better, your first creation of your mind is going to be of superior quality, and that will only lead to a high-quality second-level creation in the real world. To put it simply, your level of success can never be greater than your level of your thinking.

Everybody uses their thinking abilities quite differently, and the distinguishing factor between highly successful people and others who live a mediocre life is in their approach to thinking. Successful people use more of their minds and do so in a more effective way that supports in creating the results they want.

They are self-aware of their own thoughts and beliefs and know what is needed to enhance the quality of life and what sabotages growth. They work hard on getting their thinking clear before they can achieve massive success. As Steve Jobs rightly said, *"You have to work hard to get your thinking clean to make it simple. But it's worth it in the end because once you get there, you can move mountains."*

Let's try to understand this with the help of an example. Assume you are driving a car and you have to reach a destination pretty quickly. When you see a clear road, you will press the accelerator and increase the speed of your vehicle. Pretty obvious! But if you see someone learning to drive out of fear or maybe naivety put one foot on the accelerator and often put another on the brake despite the empty road, you already know what's going to happen. You won't reach your destination faster, and to the contrary, you will be damaging your vehicle by doing these contradictory activities. In their right minds, no one would do this to their vehicles. But, unfortunately, most people do the same thing in their inner worlds – their minds.

They try to learn and implement the best strategies and practices to achieve results – the equivalent of pressing the accelerator of our minds. But, unfortunately, they don't stand guard against the erroneous thinking patterns running through their minds due to an unsupportive environment and beliefs, which is equal to applying the brakes simultaneously while racing the car.

One of the important components of learning is to first unlearn before you learn anything new. If you realize that the old patterns of thinking don't further support and improve the quality of your decisions and your life, it's time to say goodbye to those thoughts. If you sincerely want to learn newer approaches, you can't keep clinging to past unsupportive modes of thinking and still learn a newer way.

This simple story of a rich man who reached out to a monk will help you understand the importance of unlearning for learning. The man was materially wealthy but lacked peace of mind, and this search led him to visit a monk. After reaching the monk, he started telling him what all he had read and his knowledge of various kinds of literature. Yet he still lacked mental peace and clarity of purpose in his life. The monk kept listening to him, and after few minutes, he offered the rich man some tea to get refreshed, to which the latter agreed. Now the monk handed over a cup and started slowly pouring tea in it from his kettle. As he was pouring the tea, the rich man shouted with surprise, "Hey, monk, what are you doing? The cup is already full and you are still pouring. You can't put any more into it."

Now the monk responded, "Your cup is also already full of so much knowledge, and until you empty your cup, I can't offer you anything new to learn. You have to create some space for the new material to come in."

Similarly, you too have to empty your cup to fill it with something new. You have to unlearn those past thinking errors that you will realize contradict the newer ways of thinking you are going to learn in this book.

For improving your quality of thinking, you have to follow a two-pronged approach. While you need to learn the best strategies to change your thinking for better, before that you have to become self-aware and get rid of unsupportive thinking patterns.

What You Should Expect From This Book?

You don't need to read this book any further, if you're sure about the errors in your thinking patterns and are already using more effective strategies to evaluate important life-situations and make better decisions. But if you feel that something is missing and you need guidance and better thinking models, this book will equip your mental tool box with some highly effective ways to help you think better, make better decisions and solve any problems.

Here is what you will learn from this book. You will understand the concept of how humans think in general. You will learn how you can change your thinking or beliefs regardless of your age. This book will cover the errors in your thinking patterns that are causing you unwanted stress and anxiety and leading to bad decisions. Once you are aware of the mental blocks that sabotage your progress, you will have more effective ways of thinking to make better choices. Lastly, I will cover how you can use your physiology to change your thinking and how some kinds of mental work are scientifically proven to enhance your cognitive abilities to a great extent.

--End of Preview--

Get your copy of the full book >>> *Intelligent Thinking: Overcome Thinking Errors, Learn Advanced Techniques to Think Intelligently, Make Smarter Choices, and Become the Best Version of Yourself*

My Books in <u>Personal Mastery Series</u>

1. <u>***Mindset Makeover:** Understand the Neuroscience of Mindset, Improve Self-Image, Master Routines for a Whole New Mind, & Reach your Full Human Potential*</u>

2. <u>***Level-Up Your Self-Discipline***: *Understand the Neuroscience of Self-Discipline, Control Your Emotions, Overcome Procrastination, and Achieve Your Difficult Goals*</u>

3. <u>***Trigger High Performance:** Upgrade Your Mind, Learn Effectively to Become an Expert, Activate Flow State to Take Relentless Action, and Perform At Your Best*</u>

Copyright © 2020 by Som Bathla

All rights reserved. No part of this book may be reproduced in any form without permission in writing from the author.

No part of this publication may be reproduced or transmitted in any form or by any means, mechanical or electronic, including photocopying or recording, or by any information storage and retrieval system, or transmitted by email or by any other means whatsoever without permission in writing from the author.

DISCLAIMER

While all attempts have been made to verify the information provided in this publication, the author does not assume any responsibility for errors, omissions, or contrary interpretations of the subject matter herein.

The views expressed are those of the author alone, and should not be taken as expert instruction or commands. The reader is responsible for his or her own actions.

The author makes no representations or warranties concerning the accuracy or completeness of the contents of this work and specifically disclaims all warranties, including, without limitation, warranties of fitness for a particular purpose. No warranty may be created or extended by sales or promotional materials. The advice and recipes contained herein may not be suitable for everyone. This work is sold with the understanding that the author is not engaged in rendering medical, legal or other professional advice or services. If professional assistance is required, the services of a competent professional person should be sought. The author shall not be liable for damages arising herefrom. The fact that an individual, organization, or website is referred to in this work as a citation and/or potential source of further information does not mean that the author endorses the information the individual, organization, or website may provide or recommendations they/it may make. Furthermore, readers should be aware that the Internet websites listed in this work might have changed or disappeared between when this work was written and when it is read.

Adherence to all applicable laws and regulations, including international, federal, state, and local governing professional licensing, business practices, advertising, and all other aspects of doing business in any jurisdiction in the world is the sole responsibility of the purchaser or reader.

Printed in Great Britain
by Amazon